D1291814

# What Others are Saying About
# Paul Barton and *Maximizing Internal Communication*

"Paul Barton has a firm understanding of human nature grounded in decades of experience across industries. He knows as well as anyone how to connect the executive's mind with the employees' hearts. He understands how leaders can propel an organization forward through clear, inspirational communication, and how poor communication can derail even the best of intentions. Paul relentlessly champions the idea that the best path to organizational success is communicating effectively with employees at every level—not just talking at them, but listening and learning through an ongoing process. So many companies get this wrong, and their execution falls short as a consequence. They could benefit from reading *Maximizing Internal Communication* and thinking through how having a great communications strategy that is respectful of employees and brings them along with your vision and direction can make a huge difference."

*~ Mike Bennett, Vice President, Communications,*
*Honeywell Performance Materials and Technologies*

"I've had the great fortune of working side-by-side with Paul Barton at three major companies—in the trenches and at the highest levels—tackling some of the most complex communication challenges imaginable. If you're looking for ways to bring purpose and vitality to your internal communication function and see your employees respond in ways you didn't think possible, then you too will want him by your side with *Maximizing Internal Communication*."

*~ Bruce Richardson, ABC, APR, Vice President,*
*Communications, PolyMet Mining Corp.*

"If you want to learn how to use internal communication to drive business results, read this book. Paul Barton is THE expert in internal communication, and the wisdom he imparts in *Maximizing Internal Communication* will change the way you think about communication theory, internal communication strategies and how to use them to produce meaningful, measurable benefits for employees and the bottom line."

*~ Lynne Boschee, APR, President of Calpurnia Communications and former Vice President, Corporate Communications, PetSmartCorporate*

"Paul Barton is a creative, innovative business communicator and a delight to work with. I've cited his hilarious, creative copywriting; his forward-thinking approach to the approval process; and his innovative insights on organizational voice in my workshops, articles and books. Now, thanks to *Maximizing Internal Communication*, we can all benefit from his tools, templates and proven practices."

*~ Ann Wylie, IABC Gold Quill Award-winning writer and editor, writing coach, trainer, consultant*

"At Hawaiian Airlines, I relied heavily on Paul Barton's expertise in employee communication to help create healthy internal and external communication programs. He has a thorough understanding of how to engage employees and how to construct effective employee communication campaigns. At Hawaiian, Paul was paramount in creating a culture where internal communication was at the heart of our communication strategy, in contrast to the subordinate role it plays within many companies."

*~ Al Hoffman, Owner, Hoffman Communications and former Senior Vice President of Corporate Communications and Public Affairs, Hawaiian Airlines*

"I have been a fan of Paul Barton's for 20 years. He understands communication as a culture and a process, which only incidentally involves publications, broadcasts, websites and the like. Moreover, he appreciates the fact that communication depends first and last on its credibility, and that its credibility depends first and last on authenticity. My recommendation: Listen to Paul Barton and do what he says. It will save you a lot of unnecessary migraines and ulcers and an awful lot of wasted money."

*~ Thomas J. Lee, International Consultant and Speaker,*
*www.MindingGaps.com*

"One of the daunting challenges in organizations today is getting everyone working together—heading toward the elusive common goal. Internal communication groups should play a crucial role in supporting such efforts, yet in many companies, they are not hitting the mark. Paul Barton is the most knowledgeable and capable internal communication pro I've ever met. He has a gift for devising innovative communication strategies that win over hearts as well as minds. Those interested in getting everyone heading in the same direction would benefit immensely by following Paul's ideas as presented in *Maximizing Internal* Communication."

*~ Kim McKinnon, Ph.D., Business Consultant and*
*Professor of Management at Arizona State University*

"Paul is both a passionate disciple of internal communication theory and a quintessential thought leader in its strategies and practices. *Maximizing Internal Communication* is easily the next "bible" for anyone looking to gain a deeper knowledge of internal communication and its role in enabling organizations to reach their objectives. Looking at the power of internal communication through Paul's lens is nothing short of enlightening and inspiring."

*~ Loren Yaskin, Founder, The Flip Side Communications and*
*former Manager, Internal Communications, PetSmart*

"Paul Barton is one of the most brilliant communication professionals I have ever met. He can grasp big picture strategies one minute and dive into implementation of tactics the next. He consistently develops communication processes and systems that drive meaningful business results."

*~ Lorenzo Sierra, ABC, Principal,*
*LoSierra Strategic Consulting*

"Paul is without question one of the brightest minds in the internal communication field and he has long been a thought-leader. He has a wealth of knowledge from working in a wide range of industries—yet the common denominator is always that he builds highly effective communications programs wherever he goes."

*~ Len Gutman, Director of Philanthropy,*
*Halle Heart Children's Museum*

"Paul Barton has written a book that is a welcome necessity to the field of business communication. Whether you are a student, instructor, or working professional, this guide will provide you clear direction and excellent case studies to elevate your understanding of how to communicate effectively in the moment when it is most crucial you do so."

*~ Serena Hasimoto, Ph.D., Professor of Communication,*
*Hawaii Pacific University*

"Paul Barton is a creative, innovative communications expert who has the ability quickly to identify and simplify issues and make things happen in the most challenging environments. At Phelps Dodge Corporation (now Freeport McMoran), Paul helped develop and implement a benefits communications campaign to help our employees understand and appreciate an array of very complex and sophisticated programs including the introduction of a full menu cafeteria benefits plan, which at the time was state of the art. Regardless of resources available, Paul was always able to develop and deliver creative solutions to unique communications challenges, whether targeted to the CEO, middle management or the employee operating the equipment at a mining sight."

*~ Don Lindner, Manager, Practice Leadership, World at Work and formerly Director of Total Rewards for Phelps Dodge Corporation*

"Paul Barton's ability to combine proven practices with fresh, creative, strategic ideas helps organizations solve complex communication problems—and drive new levels of employee engagement."

*~ Cathy Gedvilas, ABC, APR, Director, Corporate Communications, Sequa Corporation*

"A master of strategic communications wordplay, wit, style, tone and timing, Paul Barton unveils his practical, results-minded advice to reach new levels of organizational impact. He introduces unique and unpredictable approaches that transcend various channels, technologies and generations to guide you through your own communications journey. My most challenging, engaging and enlightening years as a communications professional have come from working alongside Paul. His heart and soul are poured into these pages. You won't be disappointed as you learn from a frontline veteran and expert in the practice of communication effectiveness."

*~ Mary Vein, Director of Marketing at Salient6 and former Director of E-Media Communications at PetSmart*

"Paul Barton's ability to combine proven practices with fresh, creative, strategic ideas helps organizations solve complex communication problems—and drive new levels of employee engagement."

"As the world of internal communications constantly changes and new technologies are introduced, Paul Barton understands how to engage employees by utilizing the right channels and resources."

"Paul Barton's holistic approach to employee communication fuses sound communication principles with speed-of-now innovation. His focus on transparency, open dialogue and value messaging is in tune with today's media savvy workforce."

"This timely book fills a void in the crisis planning and management market for professionals engaged with employee publics. Paul Barton's active learning approach uses step-by-step templates to apply communication principles to hypothetical crises, case studies and good old common sense drawn from experience. All combine to give you the tools you need to overcome the unexpected by effectively training and, if needed, using a winning internal communication team. Paul Barton will help you not only survive the next crisis but also prosper beyond it."

"Paul Barton knows what it takes to put together a winning internal communication program and you will too after reading *Maximizing Internal Communication*."

~ *Pat McGowan, Senior Project Manager, Spirit Airlines*

"Some people are simply gifted when it comes to understanding organizational communication needs and crafting messages that resonate with employees. Paul Barton is one of those people. Strong writing and editing skills developed through an early career in journalism complement his experience leading internal communication at large, complex organizations. Paul stays ahead of the curve and is often aware of new ideas, tools and trends in employee communication long before they are seen by others."

~ *Clay Allen, Director of Brand Experience, Intermountain Healthcare*

"Paul Barton provides a creative and engaging communication approach that allows for smooth rollouts of large-scale initiatives and helps speed the adoption of change by employees. This saves companies time, money and heartache."

~ *Deena W. Tearney, CEO, Pacific Point Inc.*

"Paul Barton has a keen sense of what employees need to hear in a clear, honest and concise manner. He understands how people read and interpret employee communication."

~ *Art Calderon, Human Resources Professional*

"Paul Barton truly understands what motivates employees. His thoughtful communications style encourages them to get involved and to do something that benefits the organization and themselves."

~ *Lisa Rapps, Independent Meeting & Event Planner, ANTHiLL Events LLC*

# Maximizing
## Internal
## Communication

Templates, Tools and Proven Practices

# Maximizing
# Internal
# Communication

Strategies to Turn Heads, Win Hearts,
Engage Employees and Get Results

# Paul Barton, ABC

AVIVA
PUBLISHING
New York

# Maximizing Internal Communication

Strategies that Turn Heads, Win Hearts, Engage Employees and Get Results

Published by:
Aviva Publishing
Lake Placid, NY
(518) 523-1320
www.avivapubs.com

Paul Barton, ABC
Telephone (808) 683-2422
Email: PaulBarton@Outlook.com
www.PaulBartonABC.com

ISBN Number: 978-1-940984-26-1
Library of Congress: 2014906399

Editor: Tyler Tichelaar
Cover Design: Element Design
Interior Book Design: Element Design
Jacket Photo: Kaitlyn Barton

Every attempt has been made to source properly all quotes.

Printed in the United States of America

First Edition

2 4 6 8 10 12

# Dedication

To Dad and Mom, Richard and Beverly Barton, for always supporting
and always believing in me.

To my beloved wife, Maribel, my daughters, Kaitlyn and Annamae, and my
son, Joshua, for your eternal patience and support. To my son, Matthew,
who passed away before this book was completed but who provided
inspiration nevertheless.

To all the internal communication professionals who strive every day to
help their organizations succeed and to help employees live better lives.

I love you all!

# Acknowledgments

I am fortunate to have worked alongside some of the best and brightest of the corporate communication profession. I am forever indebted to my esteemed colleagues Lynne Boschee, Bruce Richardson, Mary Vein, Loren Yaskin, Clay Allen, Lorenzo Sierra and many others from whom I learned so much, and with whom I worked and laughed so hard. Many of the applied approaches contained in this book came from the collective wisdom of this incredibly talented group of corporate communication professionals.

Special acknowledgment goes to the godfather of strategic internal communication, Roger D'Aprix, communication consultants Thomas J. Lee and Bill Hiniker, writing coach Ann Wiley, and measurement experts Angela Sinickas and Wilma Matthews for their wisdom and inspiration. Their philosophies and methodologies continue to guide me. Also, special thanks goes to the communication faculty of Hawaii Pacific University for allowing me to write the first draft of this book as the capstone project of my Master's degree.

There are many other friends, colleagues and mentors who have helped and encouraged me along the way including this partial list: Damian Balinowski, Dinah Brooks, Robert Berrier, Art Calderon, Jim Colletti, Steve and Cindy Crescenzo, Andrea Davis, Jessica Douglas, Ginette Daniels, Dave Erdman, Jennifer Erickson, Michelle Friedman, Cathy Gedvilas, Moses George, Chuck Gose, Esther Grenz, Don Griffith, Len Gutman, Serena Hashimoto, Al Hoffman, Shel Holtz, Stephanie Johnson, Kathy Kerchner, Sally Kur, Pat McGowan, Don Lindner, Kim McKinnon, Donna Mun, Barry Oleksak, Sue Oliver, Kevin Paulin, Rodney Platt, Lisa Rapps, Shana Richards, Mark Scarp, Danielle Sittu, Patrick Snow, Deena W. Tearney, James D. Whitfield and Sandra Wu. I am very grateful to you all!

# Contents

Introduction – The Noble Pursuit . . . . . . . . . . . . . . . . . . . . . . . . . .1

Chapter 1 – Making Internal Communication a Priority . . . . . . . . . . . .7

Chapter 2 – Determining the Structure and
            Role of Internal Communication . . . . . . . . . . . . . . . . . . .19

Chapter 3 – Creating Tools and Rules to Get the Job Done . . . . . . . .37

Chapter 4 – Choosing the Right Channels . . . . . . . . . . . . . . . . . . . .59

Chapter 5 – Planning Strategically . . . . . . . . . . . . . . . . . . . . . . . . .71

Chapter 6 – Finding the Voice of the Brand . . . . . . . . . . . . . . . . . .109

Chapter 7 – Communicating Employee Benefits . . . . . . . . . . . . . . .129

Chapter 8 – Communicating with Employees During a Crisis . . . . . . .143

Chapter 9 – Communicating Change to Employees . . . . . . . . . . . . .159

Chapter 10 – Evaluating Internal
             Communication Effectiveness . . . . . . . . . . . . . . . . . . .179

A Final Note - Employee Communication Nirvana . . . . . . . . . . . . . .201

20 Guiding Principles for Internal Communication . . . . . . . . . . . . . .205

About the Author . . . . . . . . . . . . . . . . . . . . . . . . . . . . . . . . . . . .209

About Paul Barton Communications, LLC . . . . . . . . . . . . . . . . . . . .211

Book Paul Barton to Speak at Your Next Event . . . . . . . . . . . . . . . .213

# A Noble Pursuit

"Everyone communicates; few connect."
– John C. Maxwell

Georg Bernard Shaw once said, "The single biggest problem in communication is the illusion that it has taken place." The same problem is absolutely true with employee communication.

Most organizations are paying far too little attention to their most important audience, their employees—and it is costing them productivity gains and profits. That's not due to a lack of information in the workplace. In fact, employees are drowning in information. They are confronted with a daily deluge of e-mails, voicemails, memos, meetings, PowerPoint presentations, teleconferences, spreadsheet reports, instructions from supervisors, workplace conversations and the never-ending din of the rumor mill. And as if that weren't enough, there are formal internal communications including company newsletters, intranets, digital signage, webcasts and corporate videos that also vie for attention.

Plenty of messages are going out—the problem is most of them aren't getting through to the people who do the work. Employees aren't being engaged in the organization's mission and vision. Although they are being drowned in information, they are left thirsting for clarity and purpose. Employees want a clear understanding of where their organizations are trying to go, how they are trying to get there and what their role is in helping their organizations succeed.

Organizations have two choices when it comes to communicating with their employees. The option they choose will determine whether they are able to engage their employees fully in the organization's success. As a communication professional, you have the opportunity to help your organization choose wisely.

Option One is to focus on communications (with an "s"), which refers to individual messages and has an emphasis on various tactics to deliver them. Option Two is to choose communication (without an "s"), which refers to an ongoing process and has an emphasis on strategies that deliver meaning and purpose. With these two options in mind, this book's purpose is to help you select Option Two so you can help your organization maximize its internal communication.

If you're reading this book, you have some interest in internal communication. You may be an internal communication professional, a corporate communication leader, in human resources or a part of your organization's leadership team. If you have responsibility over internal communication, you have an important role in your organization and this book's goal is to help you perform that role to the maximum level of effectiveness.

Before we go any further, it is important that I ask you some questions to help you make the right selection:

- Are you viewed by the leaders of your organization as someone who just sends messages out rather than as a trusted adviser?

- Does your organization tend to focus on communicating to more than with its employees?

- Are messages in your organization more about what to do than why we're doing it? Are some people in your organization focused more on outputs than on outcomes?

- Is your organization more focused on command-and-control than influence-and-include? Are communications in your organization sometimes one-off and fragmented rather than integrated and coordinated?

- Are messages in your organization sometimes lacking clear direction, prioritization and context?

- Are messages sometimes contradictory to the organization's value messages? Are most of your communication processes and procedures undocumented and improvised as situations arise?

If you answered "Yes" to any of these questions, then the solutions you seek to maximize your internal communication and begin to engage your employees can be found by reading this book.

Employees need communication that follows the Six Cs: clear, concise, consistent, coordinated, credible and compelling. They need their organizations to be open and honest and to communicate the business rationale for difficult decisions. They need organizations that value employees and are committed to communicating to them effectively. Employees are attuned to the value messages an organization sends through its working conditions, employee benefits offerings, policies and procedures, taboo topics and unwritten rules. Employees know whether an organization's actions are aligned with its value claims. They know that the attributes that get an employee hired, the accomplishments that get an employee promoted and the specific actions that can get an employee fired speak volumes about what an organization really stands for. Employees need organizations where the "do" matches the "say."

Employee communication professionals who maximize internal communication understand that employees want to feel a sense of shared purpose and shared commitment. They understand that when employees come to work, they don't leave their hearts at home. They believe that internal communication is not about telling employees what to think; it is about creating and enabling authentic, ongoing dialogues with and between them. They help organizations replace ineffective management communication models rooted in the Industrial Age with new approaches better suited for Digital Age technologies and Millennial mindsets. They create communication structures that allow for transparent top-down communication from leaders, meaningful bottom-up feedback from employees and free-flowing peer-to-peer communication among the entire workforce. They enable the conversations that allow organizations to uncover and leverage untapped knowledge from within their own workforce and achieve maximum effectiveness.

Some of you may think that maximizing internal communication in your organization is too difficult. You may be thinking, "I'm already buried in work and I don't have time to do anything else." Or you may be thinking, "Our plate is full and we don't have the staff or the budget to undertake some grandiose new plan."

Having spent nearly 20 years in corporate communications with five large companies, I understand the doubts and fears you are having. I know the frustration of having too much work, not enough support and never enough time. I know that working "a half day" means putting in 12 hours, and I know what it is like to live by the motto: "Don't stop to think or you'll miss the deadline." Sometimes you have teammates, but they're usually too busy doing their own thing to help you. Internal communication is seldom allotted anything more than a shoestring budget. Everyone in your organization thinks he or she is a communicator. And everyone wants everything yesterday.

On any given day, you could be called upon to serve as a management consultant, editor, writer, event organizer, executive speechwriter, PowerPoint guru, photographer, graphic designer, intranet content manager, or podcast interviewer. You wear many hats, but firefighter seems to be the one you wear the most as you go from extinguishing one burning issue after another. You've become very adept at juggling projects, but the priorities keep changing. You come to work with the intention of doing one thing and get pulled in an entirely different direction before lunch. You're so busy, so frustrated and so overwhelmed that sometimes you don't know where to start.

It is not easy and it does take time, but you can turn your internal communication function around, get headed in the right direction and, eventually, maximize your internal communication. I know because I've been there and done that. I have built internal communication functions from inception to successful operation, and I have rebuilt and transformed languishing internal communication efforts into highly effective programs. I've been a one-man team doing it all, and I've led internal communication teams of as many as six communication experts.

Over my corporate career, my colleagues and I developed the robust tools and templates, the rigorous practices and the enlightened strategies to maximize internal communication. Those tools, templates, practices and strategies were developed and deployed in a wide range of industries. Electric utility, mining, manufacturing, transportation, retail—each had its own unique organizational complexities and cultural considerations. The templates, tools, practices and strategies we employed were refined over and over as they were battle tested again and again by real world communication challenges including organizational restructurings, layoffs, mergers, acquisitions, union negotiations, rebranding initiatives, crises of all kinds, large-scale projects and wide-sweeping change initiatives.

This book is a roadmap to guide you on your quest to maximize your internal communication function. In these pages, I present sound communication principles and proven methodologies you can start using right away to build a foundation upon which breakthrough solutions can be created. I will show you that effective communication strategies don't necessarily require bigger budgets or the latest whiz-bang technology, and they most certainly don't presuppose that saturating employees with more and more communications will increase desired results. This book puts forth communication strategies designed to win hearts as well as minds, engage employees and attain measurable and meaningful results. By consistently delivering projects on time, on budget and on brand, and by achieving results that matter, you earn the support and autonomy you need to be a strategic communicator and a trusted executive counselor.

I challenge you to take your internal communication function to the next level. Now is the right time to begin. The opportunities for employee communicators have never been greater, and the possibilities have never been more exciting. Organizations increasingly need effective internal communication to stay competitive. We have an opportunity to show organizations how powerful internal communication strategies can drive business results. As strategic employee communicators, we can provide our organizational leaders with vision and counsel from our unique inside perspective. We can provide organizations with proven principles and communication methodologies that actively engage employees in the organization's success. We can use strategic communication to generate the creative spark that transforms a good organization into a great organization.

My goal is to help you achieve as much success in your organization as quickly as possible. I will share everything I've learned to help reduce your learning curve. When you apply the templates, tools, proven practices and strategies in this book to your day-to-day work, you ultimately will maximize your internal communication.

I believe effective internal communication is a powerful force that not only helps organizations to be more successful, but also helps enrich employees' lives in meaningful ways. By articulating the organizational vision and clarifying expectations, we help employees to have more rewarding careers. We communicate procedures that make the workplace safer. By clearly communicating employee benefits offerings, we help employees make better choices that enhance their and their loved ones' lives. We help employees understand and assimilate change, and thus reduce uncertainty and anxiety. By communicating with compassion and as a source of accurate information during times of trouble, we give employees optimism and direction. We make employees aware of available resources to help them. In these and countless other ways, we are engaged in an honorable profession that helps organizations and the people who work for them.

This is a noble pursuit! I want to inspire you to strive higher, and I want to help you by being your accountability partner.

Are you ready to begin? Do you have an open mind? Are you willing to stop looking for all the reasons why it can't be done and start looking for where we should begin? If so, let's get started!

*Paul Barton*

# Chapter 1

# Making Internal Communication a Priority

"Nothing in life is more important than the ability
to communicate effectively."
– Gerald Ford

**Chapter Overview:** Employees are an organization's most important audience, so internal communication must be a top priority if that organization is going to be successful. In this chapter, you will learn why internal communication is crucial to an organization's success. You will learn several ways that effective communication can propel organizational performance, and you will see how employees equipped with the right information can be a powerful influence on other employees' perceptions and on external audiences, especially customers. Employees aren't just the first line of defense to an organization's brand; employees are the brand.

O f all the audiences an organization communicates with, I am convinced the employee audience is the most important audience for three simple reasons:

- Employees directly impact organizational productivity, and thus, profitability.

- Employees influence one another.

- Employees influence external audience perceptions, especially those of customers, in ways that public relations and marketing efforts cannot.

The impact on performance and perception directly affects an organization's profitability. In fact, studies repeatedly have shown that the more effective an organization is at communicating with its employees, the better it performs financially.

Since 2003, Towers Watson, one of the largest consulting firms in the world, has produced a series of reports consistently showing that organizations that communicate effectively with their employees also are the best overall financial performers. Towers Watson's "Capitalizing on Effective Communication" (2009/2010) reports showed that companies that were highly effective communicators had 47% higher total returns to shareholders over a five-year period compared to companies that were the least effective communicators. ROI Communication, a consulting firm devoted to internal communication, found similar results in its "ROI Communication Benchmark" (2013) survey. The ROI survey results revealed a strong positive correlation between how open an organization's communication culture is and the organization's earnings per share (EPS).

Let's look at some specific reasons why the best communicators are also the best financial performers.

## Increasing Performance Through Engagement

Common sense tells us that better information results in better and faster decision-making, and that's certainly true for organizations communicating with their employees. What's also true is that knowing what to do correctly and being able to do it quickly enhances productivity. Employees perform the work. Therefore, if internal communication is not your organization's top priority, then all of your other priorities are at risk of not getting done correctly, efficiently, or maybe at all.

Employees need the Six Cs of communication to do their jobs efficiently. They need communication that is:

1. Clear to avoid confusion.
2. Concise because we don't have time to read.
3. Consistent so it doesn't appear to conflict with other messaging.
4. Coordinated so it doesn't get lost with other messages.
5. Credible because if we don't trust, we don't believe.
6. Compelling so we pay attention in the first place.

The Six Cs are necessary for good communication, but we have an opportunity to go even further by telling employees why they are doing what they are doing. To achieve maximum productivity from the workforce, an organization must communicate to employees the "what" and the "why" and then demonstrate how an employee's individual role contributes to the organization's overall success. The "why" doesn't have to be a lengthy explanation. Sometimes, it is as simple as adding a clause to a directive. For example, instead of writing "Remove the product from the shelf immediately," you could add, "Due to a manufacturer's safety recall, remove the product from the shelf immediately." By letting employees in on the "why," you will begin to engage them more actively in the "what." And it won't cost you a dime!

## Engaging Employees

Getting as many employees as you can to become as engaged as possible in the organization's success is a primary goal of effective internal communication.

Many things contribute to how engaged an employee is with his or her organization: how receptive the organizational culture is to engagement, how successful the organization is, how satisfied employees are with their salary and working conditions, how proud they are of their organization, how well they understand how their jobs contribute to the organization's success, and how well they understand where the organization is trying to go and how it is trying to get there. Effective internal communication can positively affect each of those areas and help to engage employees in the organization's success. Conversely, an organization without effective internal communication can never achieve its full potential. Even if that organization is doing well, it could do better with more effective internal communication and more engaged employees. A lack of effective internal communication could mean the difference between an organization being good and an organization being great.

Most organizations have mixed levels of employee engagement. There are those employees who are "all in" for the organization. Other employees are engaged some of the time and other times not so much. It may be "just a job" for some. Some employees may have become disillusioned and are seeking other job opportunities. And there may even be a few employees who are actively working to undermine the organization. Renowned internal communication consultant Roger D'Aprix says the more engaged an employee is, the more he will talk of "we." The less engaged an employee is, the more he will talk about "me." Effective internal communication can help engage employees and move those focused on "me" to "we" (D'Aprix, 2009). Totally engaged employees bring many benefits to an organization including:

- Engaged employees are more satisfied with their jobs and that reduces attrition, which saves an organization from the costs of recruiting and training new employees, and from the costs of lost productivity while new employees get up to speed.

- Engaged employees work harder, smarter and safer. They are dedicated to success and will do what it takes to get the job done. They are often more creative in problem-solving and the overall approach to their jobs. They improve the quality of products and services. They follow established procedures and work safer, which saves lost labor costs and, more importantly, human lives. They go above and beyond their job duties to help colleagues and customers.

- Engaged employees embrace new and better ways to do their jobs. They understand the need for change. They initiate and foster change. They trust their leaders. They are eager to learn more and eager to share information with one another. They take on new responsibilities. They are in a continuous-improvement mode. Instead of blaming others, they seek root causes for problems and they solve them. They celebrate successes and they are more tolerant when things aren't going so well for the business.

In short, engaged employees are more productive. But there's even more good news. Engaged employees also can be "Cultural Warriors" who influence internal audiences and "Brand Champions" who influence external audiences.

## Inspiring Cultural Warriors

Modern organizations need to respond and adapt quickly to survive. They continuously need to improve productivity and quality and do so increasingly faster to stay competitive. At all five corporations where I worked, some change or another was always afoot. Organizations often find they must change the way they operate their business and do so in wide-sweeping ways. Maybe they're trying to improve operational performance or customer service. They may need to change technologies or system processes. Maybe they're trying to assimilate change as the result of a merger or acquisition. They may need to change to comply with new laws or regulations. Whatever the reason necessitating the change, organizations will find that engaged employees who are already bought-in to an organization's business objectives and the company vision are much more prone to jump on board with that organization's efforts to transform.

Because engaged employees can help influence other employees who are not yet aligned with a particular change effort, I refer to them as "Cultural Warriors." These employees can be an important target audience to communicate with as part of a communication plan that includes change management. Notice the use of the term communicate with rather than communicate to. Cultural Warriors need to be part of the change process by serving on focus groups or as part of task teams that help formulate the change strategy. Then, armed with communications that are credible, candid and complete, these Cultural Warriors can help persuade other employees to accept the change. Think about it this way: if an organization can't get its most engaged employees to support a change effort, it likely will have little success getting neutral employees on board and probably no chance whatsoever of getting skeptical employees to go along with the change.

## Creating Brand Champions

Engaged employees also can influence external audiences. In fact, the more effective internal communication is, the less an organization needs to rely on its external communication efforts. That's because employees equipped with the right information can become "Brand Champions" for an organization. This army of advocates also can become an effective external communication channel.

This aspect of internal communication is another reason why many believe the employee audience is an organization's most important audience. Communication consultant Shel Holtz put it this way: "The employee audience is the most important because it can undermine the best communication effort or overcome the worst." (Holtz, 2004).

For retail and service-oriented businesses, frontline employees are the face of those organizations to their customers. They are not just the first line of defense for a brand; they are the brand as far as customers see it. An organization can project a brand image through its public relations and marketing campaigns, but it is the interaction between employees and customers, the interactions employees have with one another that customers observe and the actual experiences that customers have with an organization that prove whether that brand image is authentic or just another advertising slogan.

## Building Brands Inside Out

Authentic brands are built from the inside out, and effective internal communication is crucial to branding success. I believe the best way to build an authentic brand starts with hiring people who already embody some of the brand's characteristics, and then reinforcing the brand through training, appropriate policies and ongoing internal communication. A brand must be authentic if the messages sent out by investor relations, public relations and marketing to their external audiences are to be believed. Brands become authentic when their claims align with the actual customer experience. The interaction between an employee and a customer is often that proof point. It is hard to imagine that employees can effectively engage customers unless they are first engaged themselves with their organization.

Think about a company you are familiar with that has a really strong brand. Now think about your own interactions with that company's employees. If the company has a strong brand, that company's employees most likely "live the brand" and make the brand authentic. Think about the interactions between employees that you observe. If employees are working cooperatively, supporting and smiling at one another, the brand imagine is enhanced. If employees smile at customers but grouse at each other, the brand image suffers, and if they are rude to each other and their customers, the brand is undermined.

Most people agree that Southwest Airlines is a company that is true to its brand image. Southwest's marketing and advertising efforts tout fun as part of their brand, and they project an image of doing business differently than other airlines. Do the employees of Southwest Airlines live up to that brand promise? You bet they do. Consider this example from my personal experience. When my son Matthew was 9 years old, he broke his arm just a week before we flew to Disney World for vacation. As we boarded our

Southwest Airlines flight, the flight crew noticed Matthew's cast and asked whether they could sign it. Every flight attendant, the captain and the first officer all signed the cast. The captain invited Matthew into the cockpit and had him sit in the captain's chair to sign his cast. He noticed how articulate Matthew was and invited him to make the "Welcome Aboard" cabin announcement over the PA system. These simple acts cost the airline nothing, but they cemented Southwest's brand image in the minds of our family and everyone else on that flight forever. Similar acts repeated over and over by employees on flight after flight make the airline's brand image authentic and make customers fiercely loyal to Southwest. Matthew was so inspired that he later learned how to fly an airplane himself.

## Influencing Customers

Effective internal communication can help create and sustain Brand Champions, and that can boost profitability. The correlation is simple: effective internal communication creates Brand Champions who create engaged customers who in turn create more sales and bigger profits.

To be effective, Brand Champions need information. Consider this fictitious example (based in part on a true story): The ABC Pet Supply Company's corporate headquarters provided employees in its stores with clear instructions about how to set up a large display in each store to sell dog collars and leads. But store employees wondered why their company had to carry so many collars and leads of every color and texture under the sun. Store managers were concerned about how much retail space the display required and the floor employees complained that the large display took a long time to set up. The employees knew exactly what to do, but they didn't know why they were doing it. They set up the display, but over the next few weeks, sales of collars and leads were mediocre. Through a previously established feedback process, comments regarding the display filtered up from the store director to the district manager and eventually to the chief operating officer. It was clear the store employees didn't understand the marketing strategy behind the display. But then, how could they understand? They had been told what to do but not why they were doing it.

The employee communicators were brought in to help. Working with the store management team, they drafted message points for store directors to share with their store employees during the morning start-up meetings that every store held. The start-up meetings had been held for the past several years and often included messages from the corporate office designed to help explain company strategies. The message points explained the rationale for the display: Marketing research showed that the company's target audience (female, 25 to 35 years old, upper income, prone to dote on their pets) bought dog collars and leads primarily as a fashion accessory, not just as a necessity. The customers wanted variety, lots of variety. Other stores, including Walmart and Target, carried some collars and leads, but did not have as much variety. Once they understood the business strategy, store employees approached customers with a new attitude. They understood what they were doing and why they were doing it. They began to interact with customers with comments such as "This collar matches your purse, and, of course, you'll want the matching leash as well."

> Without adequate information, even an organization's strongest employee advocates can be left speechless.

Sales of collars and leads increased dramatically over the next few months and so did customer satisfaction. Customers were willing to pay a little more for collars and leads because they appreciated the wide variety and because they felt the store employees understood their needs better. Another benefit of this effective internal communication was increased employee job satisfaction. Once employees understood what the sales strategy was and how important their role was, they were no longer complaining about the display's size or the amount of time it took to set it up. They were eager to learn more and to share the information with others.

## Influencing Other External Audiences

In addition to customer interactions, Brand Champions can help spread the word about an organization to family members, friends, neighbors, and others in the community and beyond. In many instances, Brand Champions have unique credibility with external audiences that make their messages highly effective. Have you ever heard something about a company in the news and then asked someone you knew who worked at that company for his opinion on the matter? If that employee worked for an organization with good communication, he probably gave you an answer that helped you understand the issue better. Brand Champions can facilitate understanding and promote organizational messages to external audiences, and those audiences can then spread the word to people they know and so on and so on.

Brand Champions can help organizations in their recruiting efforts to attract and retain the best and brightest talent available. After all, who doesn't want to work for an organization with happy, highly motivated employees?

When a crisis or controversy strikes a company, Brand Champions can defend their organization in more credible ways than public relations and marketing messaging. Given the right information, Brand Champions can have a significant influence. But without adequate information, even an organization's strongest employee advocates can be left speechless.

Here's another example from my personal experience that illustrates the power of arming employees with messaging. The Environmental Protection Agency made a change in which minerals it was going to include on its annual Toxic Release Inventory (TRI) report. That change would cause our company, the nation's largest copper mining company, to go from not being on the TRI list at all to being at the top of the list. Fearing the news media would misunderstand the information and create dramatic headlines touting Phelps Dodge as the nation's top polluter once the change went into effect, we decided to get out in front of the issue by telling our side of the story first. We crafted messaging for the news media, key public officials, and our own shareholders and employees. We created press releases, fact sheets, letters and newsletters.

The company wanted to enable its employee Brand Champions to help carry its messages. We recognized that many of our employees were second and third generation miners. Mining was in their blood. They were eager to defend what they did for a living. We already had communicated the TRI change to all of our employees through company newsletters and team meetings. But we decided to go a step further. We created a wallet-sized fact sheet that our employees could carry with them and use to discuss the facts about the TRI across their neighbor's fence, in the grocery aisle or wherever they were. The fact sheet allowed employees to tell the company's side of the story.

> Virtually any employee can create a website, a blog or an e-mail newsletter, and any employee with a smartphone can access social media sites and participate in discussions about his or her company at any time.

The dramatic headlines never materialized, perhaps because the company was able to get out in front of the controversy and educate the news media and community. Employees felt that much more committed to the company. After all, we had trusted them to help carry an important message. And, in doing so, we sent a subtle message to our employees— we're all in this together.

## Creating an External Communication Policy

Organizations need to understand that whether or not they cultivate Brand Champions, employees are going to talk about their organizations to external audiences. At the very least, they are going to talk to their families and friends. And through letters to the editor in newspapers and magazines, call-in talk radio shows, and social media channels and other web-based applications, employees have the potential to reach large numbers of people with their thoughts about their own organizations. Virtually any employee can create a website, a blog or an e-mail newsletter, and any employee with a smartphone can access social media sites and participate in discussions about his or her company at any time. Whether messages are positive or negative largely depends on how engaged the employee is with the organization and how well the organization has communicated with the employee. Some organizations still believe they can tightly control messages through company spokespeople, but that is no longer the case, if it ever really was.

Some organizations encourage their employees to participate in external social media channels as a way to extend their brands. For example, Best Buy encourages every employee to be actively engaged on Twitter. Former Best Buy CEO Brian Dunn said the reward his company reaped by allowing his employees to Tweet far outweighed the risk of them saying something inappropriate. "Playing it safe is the riskiest thing communicators can do," said Dunn (Dunn, B. 2009).

Given that employees can take their messages to mass audiences, I advise organizations to create a written external communication policy for employees. While the best strategy is to engage employees as much as possible and provide them with the best information, care must be taken not to let such a strategy run amok. An external communication policy for employees should cover who can talk to the news media and who can communicate on public forums, including social media, and under what conditions. A sample external communication policy for employees is contained in Chapter 8. It is presented there as a tool to aid organizations during a crisis situation.

## Chapter Conclusion

Internal communication can do far more than just impart marching orders from management to the rank and file. In fact, if your intent is simply to impart information, you're just disseminating news and not really communicating at all. But by engaging employees through effective communication, your organization can help expand its brand, boost its financial performance and position itself for long-term success.

Given that so many organizations underestimate the importance of their employee audience, organizations that choose to focus on maximizing their internal communication could gain a solid competitive advantage. Effective internal communication just might be your organization's secret weapon.

## Chapter Exercises

1. Write a definition for "Cultural Warrior" and a definition for "Brand Champion."

_____
_____
_____
_____
_____
_____
_____
_____
_____
_____
_____
_____
_____

2. Write a description of an interaction you had with a company's employees that affected your perception of that company's brand.

_____
_____
_____
_____
_____
_____
_____
_____
_____
_____
_____
_____

## Chapter References

D'Aprix, R. (2009). *The Face-to-Face Communication Toolkit: Creating An Engaged Workforce*. San Francisco: International Association of Business Communicators (IABC)

Dunn, B. (2009) *"Engaging Employees."* International Association of Business Communicators (IABC), San Francisco. June 10, 2009.

Holtz, S. (2004). *Corporate Conversations: A Guide to Crafting Effective and Appropriate Internal Communications*. New York: AMACOM.

# Chapter 2

# Determining the Structure and Role of Internal Communication

"Put it before them briefly so they will read it, clearly so they will appreciate it, picturesquely so they will remember it, and above all, accurately so they will be guided by its light."
– Joseph Pulitzer

**Chapter Overview:** In this chapter, you'll learn about a powerful strategic vision that will help you determine exactly what it is you are aspiring to achieve in your role as an internal communication professional. Just as in any transformation project, understanding where you are right now and knowing where you're headed is crucial to getting there. This chapter traces the journey from tactician and "fast food communicator" to strategic communicator and executive counselor.

The internal communication function can be cast in a supporting role or in a leading role depending on how the organization values the function and what is needed. Whatever their role, employee communicators typically need to wear many different hats. On any given day, an employee communicator may be a management consultant, editor, writer, event organizer, speechwriter, PowerPoint presentation guru, photographer, graphic designer, intranet content manager or podcast interviewer. The employee communicator may be leading a communication initiative, or providing communication support to an internal client or as a member of a cross-functional project task team.

# Structuring

Internal communication can be handled by one person or by a team of communicators. The team's size is not necessarily determined by the size of the organization. Some very large organizations have only a few people dedicated to internal communication while some relatively small organizations have many people dedicated to it. The team's size likely depends on how the organization views the scope of the internal communication function. For example, a large global corporation may have only one or two people dedicated to internal communication at the headquarters level because the organization's leaders see the function as only responsible for communicating messages emanating from the corporate headquarters. Other internal communications in such a company might be handled at the local level or by other departments. It is common to find the human resources staff at each local location responsible for producing an employee newsletter for its worksite.

In some cases, an organization will have highly trained personnel dedicated solely to internal communication, or it may have responsibilities for both internal and external communications. These individuals likely will have college degrees in organizational communication, public relations, journalism or some other communication-related degree. Many also will be members of a professional association such as the International Association of Business Communicators (IABC) or the Public Relations Society of America (PRSA). Both associations offer seminars and conferences related to internal communication and certifications. IABC tends to focus more on internal communication.

While some internal communicators are highly trained and stay current by attending numerous communication seminars and conferences, others may have little or no training in the field. In some cases, internal communication is just one of many responsibilities handled by a particular individual who may not have received any formal communication training. For instance, human resources generalists are often tasked with employee communication in addition to their regular duties. They may be responsible for creating newsletters and other internal communication collateral materials.

# Reporting Relationships

The internal communication function may be part of a larger corporate communication team or it may be part of another department, such as human resources. The reporting relationship of the internal communication function is often quite telling about how the organization views the internal communication role. If the organization is a corporation that highly values overall communication, it likely has a corporate communication department and the internal communication function likely is part of that team. A vice president or a senior vice president of corporate communication leads most corporate communication teams. The corporate communication function can report directly to the CEO or through another department such as marketing, human resources or legal.

Where the organization chooses to have corporate communication report can say a lot about where the organization's priorities are and how it values communication. For instance, a leadership team that has its vice president of corporate communication reporting directly to the CEO likely sees communicators as executive counselors, or at least as direct support for such tasks as the development of key messages, speechwriting and presentations. A leadership team that has its vice president of corporate communication reporting directly to the chief legal counsel may be primarily concerned with communications dealing with product litigation or collective-bargaining agreements and labor unions.

Typically, a corporate communication team is divided between external and internal responsibilities. External responsibilities include public relations and may include investor relations and other specialty areas. Internal communication may include executive communication to employees, broad-based employee communication, employee benefit communication and other internal specialty areas. For instance, a large airline might have a communicator focused on just pilot communication or a large retailer may have a communicator dedicated solely to communication to its store managers. As previously mentioned, many professional communicators will have responsibilities for both internal and external communication.

Traditionally, organizations have been concerned primarily with their external image, and therefore, the emphasis is often on the PR side of the house and less on the internal communication function. The vast majority of vice presidents of corporate communication rise from the PR ranks. Communication budgets typically have more funding for external initiatives than for internal communication projects. The organization frequently will retain outside PR agencies to assist with the external communication workload but may be more reluctant to do the same for internal communication projects. Colleges and universities typically emphasize PR over internal communication in their course offerings. Internal communication is often just a single chapter in a textbook on organizational communication. Many students emerging from universities with communication degrees hope to land a PR job but end up settling for an internal communication position as an entry point. This lopsided emphasis on PR is gradually changing as internal communication continues to prove its ability to impact organizational success and as the work performed by employee communicators becomes more meaningful.

## Identifying Communication Partners

Wherever employee communicators report and however their teams are structured, they likely will find themselves partnering frequently with individuals in other departments such as training, employee benefits, organizational change, safety, legal and information technology. The employee communicators may offer communication support to other departments ranging from advice on effective communication strategies to drafting the communication materials for them.

Some departments may from time to time engage in activities that are in essence employee communication; however, the various leaders of those departments may not see them as such. After all, we're all communicators; we're just not all professionally trained as such. The safety department may produce its own newsletters, posters and videos, and it may distribute items containing safety messages on them such as coffee mugs, pens, etc. It is not uncommon for the safety communication budget to be much larger than the internal communication budget.

Sometimes other departments will hire outside vendors to provide communication expertise in a given area. Ideally in such situations, the internal communication function will partner with the department and its outside vendors to ensure messages are consistent with larger organizational messages, that communications are "on brand" and that the timing of message distribution is coordinated with other organizational messages.

# Internal Communication vs. Employee Communication

Throughout this book, you'll see the terms "internal communication" and "employee communication." They are not necessarily used interchangeably. I try to use the term best-suited to the context. No agreement exists among communication professionals as to the exact definition of the two terms, but there is a clear preference for "internal." While it may not seem like a terribly important question, it is one that generates interest and a bit of passion among communication professionals. When I posed the question on my blog and several LinkedIn group discussions, I received more than 100 responses. Figure 2.1 shows some of the two terms' advantages and disadvantages that I distilled from the online comments I received.

**Figure 2.1: Internal Communication or Employee Communication**

| | EMPLOYEE COMMUNICATION | INTERNAL COMMUNICATION |
|---|---|---|
| **Advantages** | • Sounds less formal and more human.<br>• More easily understood by those outside the profession. | • More inclusive of other internal groups.<br>• More descriptive of the function. |
| **Disadvantages** | • Sounds too top-down and one-directional. | • Confused with internal telecommunications by those not familiar with the profession. |
| **Other Comments** | • Not used as much outside the U.S.<br>• Many feel employee communication is a subset of internal communication.<br>• Refers to people. | • Overwhelmingly preferred by professional communicators worldwide.<br>• Refers to a place, not people. |

Whether we're called internal communication or employee communication, the most important thing is, of course, that we're doing a great job and contributing in meaningful ways to the long-term success of our organizations and the well-being of our internal audiences.

# Crafting a Strategic Vision for the Internal Communication Team

Internal communication teams can come in many different shapes and sizes and have a wide range of responsibilities. A highly successful internal communication team is the eyes, ears and internal voice of its organization. Highly effective employee communicators are the strategic communication counselors for the organization's leadership. They help those in charge to see their role as leaders and not just managers, and they help them to understand that leadership and communication are one and the same. The internal communication team members serve as internal consultants, facilitators and resource partners to help their organization achieve its business objectives by developing and executing effective communication strategies.

Many employee communicators are cast in tactical support roles, and they find themselves struggling to achieve a more strategic role in their organization so they can make a greater impact. Figure 2.2 shows the various roles employee communicators may find themselves in.

**Figure 2.2: Employee Communicator Roles**

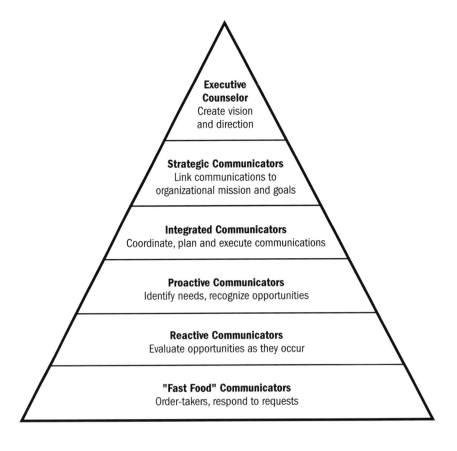

**Fast Food Communicators:** At the bottom of the pyramid are Fast Food Communicators. Those cast in that role wait for communication requests to come to them and then react to them by creating information and disseminating it. Many of them become quite adept at fulfilling requests quickly and accurately, and their internal clients often report high satisfaction with the job they are performing. But the communication they produce often doesn't produce the best results possible because they lack strategy and integration with other communication opportunities.

The internal client who is not a professional communicator and may not even be aware of other more effective communication channels or more effective strategic approaches often decides the communication channel to be used. For example, internal clients often suggest lengthy newsletter articles as the solution to their communication challenge because it is the channel with which they are most familiar. The longer the article, the better because it will have more impact, they incorrectly reason. They'll pepper articles with manufactured quotes from management using all the buzzwords that will please the organization's senior leadership. The communication team may turn around this request very quickly, and the internal client may be very pleased with its work. The work may be just what the internal client wants, but it may not be what he actually needs. The result most likely won't be as impactful as it could have been with a strategic multi-channel coordinated campaign approach. What's more, the client most likely won't know whether the communication was effective or not because the "Fast Food" approach probably didn't include any measurement plan to determine success.

Fast Food communications are typically fragmented and uncoordinated. The inconsistent tone and format inherent in such ad-hoc communications creates many voices all vying for attention. Priorities are unclear. Instead of seeing how each individual organizational initiative is part of a larger plan, the "one-off" approach of Fast Food communications creates the perception that a hundred unrelated projects are going on simultaneously. Fast Food communications create a climate of confusion and contribute to employees feeling overwhelmed. Typically, the "Fast Food Approach" doesn't target specific audiences with tailored messages and doesn't include feedback mechanisms.

The type of information communicated in the "Fast Food" approach typically falls into one of the following categories:

- **Data Reports:** Typically data are presented in a spreadsheet report. Such reports usually lack any context as to why the data are important and how they relate to the big picture of what the organization is trying to achieve.

- **Directives:** Directive information often is presented as step-by-step instructions on what to do, but it usually lacks why the action is being requested and how the action ties to larger organizational priorities.

- **Informational Messages:** Informational messages typically are presented in an objective news tone, which lacks context and credibility because no one believes the organization's leadership is actually objective.

In the fast-paced environment most organizations are in, it is tempting just to react to what internal clients want and to keep them happy. In most cases, internal clients are simply unaware how much effective communication can do for them. In addition, they may be unaware of how a specific communication could be tied to a larger communication strategy and help support broader organizational goals. Being helpful to these internal clients in their short-term requests might actually be doing them and the overall organization a disservice in the long run.

**Reactive Communicators:** Internal communication teams seeking to break out of the "Fast Food" approach usually do so in incremental steps. The next step up from "Fast Food Communicators" is "Reactive Communicators," who don't always wait to be told when or how to communicate, but they still find that they are reacting to events as they unfold. Reactive Communicators can become very good at evaluating opportunities as they occur, but they will still fall short of maximum effectiveness. They are, however, poised to reach the next level, "Proactive Communicators."

**Proactive Communicators:** At this level, the communicators are adept at identifying needs and recognizing opportunities. They likely are still fulfilling a lot of lower level reactive communication requests as well, but they take a more proactive approach to more meaningful projects and thus position themselves to move up to the next level, "Integrated Communicators."

**Integrated Communicators:** At this level, the communicators are coordinating various communication channels to work together on messaging. They are likely partnering with other teams to ensure consistent messages are disseminating throughout the organization. They may perform highly visible tasks for senior leadership such as producing charts and PowerPoint presentations. They are making a more meaningful impact than ever before, but more still needs to be done for maximum effectiveness.

In the first three levels of the pyramid, the emphasis is on the tactics involved in getting information out and not on the strategy of getting information through. The measurement in this phase is most likely on the tactics, such as how many newsletter articles were produced, and not on the measurable impact of the communication. Those who are focused on tactical communications are more interested in the saturation of messages than on their effectiveness. They value activity over actual results. It is difficult for teams to break out of these tactical levels for numerous reasons, including a heavy workload and demands by internal clients who are often seeking a "silver bullet" to solve their communication challenge. Internal clients often believe a single communication channel such as a video, a payroll stuffer or a newsletter article can fulfill complex communication challenges such as improving employee morale or gaining employee acceptance of an important organizational change.

**Strategic Communicators:** Over time, with patience, perseverance and by consistently demonstrating value and showing measurable, quantifiable results, employee communicators can move to the Strategic Communicator level where the communication strategies are clearly linked to the organization's mission. Strategic communicators combine planning and action. They develop written communication strategies and constantly seek to improve upon those plans. If they don't have a large enough staff to do everything, they choose projects that are meaningful to the organization's leaders. When they engage in a meaningful project, they produce measurable results. They make time to plan and think about what they are doing. They use their plans to set priorities and guide their daily work. They focus on what's important, not just what's urgent. They use communication strategies to solve non-communication challenges the business is facing and the organization's leaders believe are important (Bill Hiniker, Message Point Communications, personal communication, July 15, 2013).

Strategic Communicators often act as internal consultants. They speak the language of their business and understand what factors drive success in the organization. They approach every internal client meeting with intellectual humility. They seek input from their clients and respect the expertise they bring to the process. They engage in active listening, and they listen more than they talk. They listen to understand, not to respond. At the same time, they take every opportunity to educate their clients about the value of their work and they provide compelling evidence. They keep the organization's senior leadership abreast of new technologies and new approaches to employee communication.

As shown in Figure 2.3, strategic communicators focus on not just what's urgent, but also on what's important, and they prioritize accordingly. But, as writing coach Ann Wylie points out, sometimes what's important isn't particularly interesting. The job of the employee communicator is to make the important interesting. Remember the Six Cs listed back in Chapter 1? No. 6 was "compelling," and making what's interesting also important is yet another way of looking at that.

Strategic communicators gain credibility by focusing on what their organization's leaders believe are important and by calling their attention to what they may not be aware of that also may be important.

**Figure 2.3: Prioritizing Strategically**

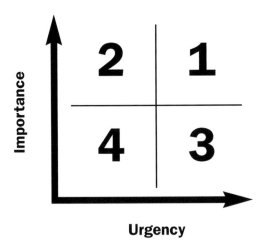

**Executive Counselors:** Over time, Strategic Communicators position themselves at the top of the pyramid as "Executive Counselors." In this role, they help create the organization's vision and help set the direction. They have a seat at the decision table, and they offer advice from an internal communication perspective on important matters to the organization. They are constantly thinking about questions such as:

- How will employees react to this news?
- What questions will they have?
- Will the message be credible to them?
- Will it be understandable?
- What will employees perceive to be the takeaways?
- What does the organization want employees to tell their family, friends and neighbors?
- What else is going on in the organization that might affect employee perceptions about the communication?

Achieving the "Executive Counselor" level doesn't mean communicators are no longer performing day-to-day tactical work. But it does mean those routine tactics are done in support of broader communication strategies. Even simple, seemingly insignificant communications can contain a branded look and language that supports larger organizational strategies. In fact, it is the repetition of communication in even the smallest of tactics that helps make the strategies work.

When internal communicators reach the top level of the pyramid, they are performing many tactical and strategic functions all at once. In a broad sense, they are (1) integrating all communication activities, (2) formulating processes and procedures for effective communication and (3) partnering with the organization's leadership and other functional areas to provide a broad range of communication services.

Following is a list of activities the internal communication function might engage in under each of these areas.

**(1) Integrating all communication activities.** The internal communication team does this by:

- Integrating key business strategies into all organization-wide communications.

- Using key business strategies as a way to filter and prioritize messages.

- Creating appropriate communication channels to ensure the timely, accurate and candid flow of information.

- Reducing communication clutter by eliminating unnecessary communications, consolidating communications when appropriate and coordinating communications to ensure consistent messaging and appropriate timing.

- Helping to shape employee attitudes and opinions about the organization.

- Communicating clear objectives and what actions are to be taken by employees.

- Personalizing messages so employees understand how their contributions and commitment can contribute to the organization's success.

- Helping to drive brand behavior by telling stories that reflect desired culture.

- Synthesizing and articulating messages so they are clearly understood and relevant.

- Providing employees with information so they can be Brand Champions for their organization.

- Helping employees to assimilate and embrace continuous change.

- Helping employees to know what resources are available to them. For example, making sure employees have all the information they need to make the most appropriate choices for themselves and their families when selecting their Employee Benefit offerings.

**(2) Formulating processes and procedures for effective communication.** The internal communication team does this by:

- Creating written communication strategies and detailed action plans, evaluating their effectiveness and continuously improving upon them.

- Consistently meeting deadlines or renegotiating them well in advance.
- Creating templates, checklists and approval and fact-checking processes that help enhance the quality, speed and accuracy of communications.
- Continually developing new skills, adapting new technologies and adding new resources.
- Identifying and understanding the organization's key audiences. Employee communicators must understand the demographics of their audiences and know which communication channels reach which groups most effectively.
- Assessing the organizational climate. This can be achieved in a variety of ways, including formal methods such as surveys and focus groups, and by collecting informal anecdotal feedback.
- Creating a common language and establishing an appropriate communication tone that reflects the organization's brand. The internal communication team may create a written style guide to help with these efforts.
- Creating a cohesive look and feel to all broad-based communications. The internal communication group may work with the marketing team to create written brand guidelines to help ensure compliance.
- Measuring the effectiveness of communication channels and specific communications and making appropriate changes if needed to enhance the channels or to refresh and recast messages.

**(3) Partnering with the organization's leadership and other functional areas to provide a broad range of communication services.** The internal communication team does this by:

- Meeting regularly with organizational leaders to understand what drives the overall business and what is important to individual departments.
- Engaging in active listening to obtain feedback from organizational leaders and internal clients and respecting their areas of expertise.
- Advising and counseling organizational leaders.
- Working with their internal clients to devise effective communication strategies.

- Coordinating graphic design and audiovisual production for internal clients.

- Coordinating and publicizing large employee events.

- Coordinating key employee messages with external messaging. Marketing messages and messaging to the news media must be consistent with employee messaging.

- Facilitating three-way communication within the organization (as shown in Figure 2.4). This includes facilitating communication from an organization's leadership to its employees, facilitating meaningful employee feedback to the organization's leaders, and facilitating communication within and between project teams, departments and individual employees to increase information sharing and enhance organizational knowledge.

Figure 2.4 is reprinted from my blog and it explains the concept of three-way communication in more detail.

**Figure 2.4: Three-Way Communication**

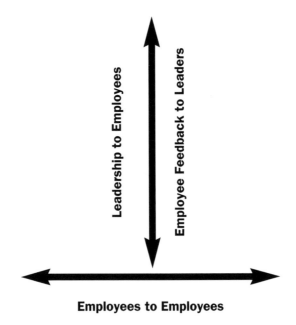

**Employees to Employees**

# Unleash the Conversations and Untap the Knowledge

Enlightened leaders know that if they unleash the conversations within their workforce, they can untap vast reservoirs of knowledge and spawn innovation. Organizations need effective communication from top to bottom, from bottom to top and from side to side. For internal communication professionals, this means facilitating:

(1) communication from an organization's leadership to its employees

(2) meaningful employee feedback to the organization's leaders

(3) communication within and between project teams, departments and individual employees to increase information sharing and collaboration.

**An old model with new technology is still an old model.** Unfortunately, many organizations still employ a top down communication system. Some fool themselves into thinking they are using a modern communication model because they use new technologies to carry their corporate messages. But a CEO webcast that doesn't have a built-in way to collect meaningful feedback, or an intranet filled with management information that doesn't allow for robust peer-to-peer information sharing or collaboration are still top-down systems.

**Two monologues don't make a dialogue.** Some organizations think they have a two-way communication model because they have an annual pulse survey or some high-tech equivalent of a suggestion box. But if feedback mechanisms aren't integrated into all communication processes and if the feedback collected isn't meaningful to the organization's leaders, then such organizations aren't really engaging in a dialogue.

**Employees come for information, but they stay for the conversation.** Employees log on to intranets seeking information, but what keeps them engaged are the conversations that occur when intranets contain collaboration technology and social media platforms that facilitate peer-to-peer communication. However, many organizational leaders are fearful such technology will be productivity killers. They cringe at the thought of employees on Yammer and they direct their IT teams to shutoff the My Site feature of SharePoint.

**If organizations only knew what they knew.** Organizations that communicate well top down can be good. Those that collect meaningful feedback are better. And those that untap the enormous knowledge base within their organization by facilitating information sharing and collaboration are the best. Unleash the conversation and find out what your organization knows.

*Reprinted from PaulBartonABC.com*

## Chapter Conclusion

Organizations seeking to maximize internal communication will have to ensure their internal communication teams are structured, staffed and funded properly to achieve their communication goals and business objectives, and that their employee communicators have enough autonomy that they are able to serve as strategic communicators and executive counselors.

You have to work hard to earn support and autonomy. You do so by building credibility and trust project-by-project, client-by-client, day-by-day. You do so by consistently delivering work that is on time, on budget and on brand. The remaining chapters in this book will help you build credibility and trust by giving you the tools and templates that facilitate flawless execution and by providing you the practices and strategies that drive meaningful business results.

## Chapter Exercises

1. Those who are focused on tactical communications are typically more focused on what?

_____

_____

2. What does a data report lack that makes it an ineffective communication?

_____

_____

3. If an internal communication team is to be successful, it must contribute what?

_____

_____

## Chapter 3

# Creating Tools and Rules to Get the Job Done

"You can do almost anything with soup stock; it's like a
strong foundation. When you have the right foundation,
everything tastes good."
– Martin Yan

**Chapter Overview:** In this chapter, you'll learn the importance
of developing appropriate "tools and rules" to support the internal
communication function. Calendars, templates, checklists, and written
processes and procedures are all necessary to get the job done
efficiently and flawlessly, and stylebooks, glossaries and branding
guidelines can help drive consistency and desired brand behavior.

Together, all of these tools help you to produce work that is on time,
on budget and on message. The tools allow you to plan the work,
rather than having the work plan you. They also help you to get out
in front of the work and operate as a strategic communicator and executive
counselor, and less as a tactician and "fast food communicator." Of course,
you will need to tailor these tools to suit your needs and develop others
depending on your organization's needs.

In a perfect world, you would first spend time developing the tools you
need to do your job and then begin serving your organization. However, in
the real world, you usually develop these tools in the midst of performing
your ongoing daily duties and while juggling multiple major projects. You
may find yourself overwhelmed with work and feel you don't have time to
develop tools. I used to feel that way until I discovered that taking the time
to develop such tools saves time in the long run, facilitates continuous

improvement, and provides a solid foundation that allows creativity and strategic thinking to flourish.

I discovered the power of a written communication plan early in my career when I had to devise a plan for a layoff at a manufacturing plant. The particular challenge with this situation was that eight different languages were spoken at the facility where the layoffs were to occur. I had never developed a plan for a layoff before, so I wasn't quite sure where to start. Imagine my joy when I came across a written strategic communication plan that had been created for a previous layoff in our online communication plan library. It had key messages, strategies and tactics I could easily adapt for my plan. It had special audiences listed (such as vendors who would be concerned about the plant potentially closing) that I might have missed. It even had a WARN letter already drafted and approved by the legal department. (The Worker Adjustment and Retraining Notification Act or "WARN" requires most employers with 100 or more employees to provide written notification 60 calendar days in advance of plant closings and mass layoffs.) The communication plan and WARN letter saved me hours of work. That gave me time to focus on ways to tackle the unique problem of my plan: the multiple language barriers. Working with the plant manager, we were able to identify trusted bilingual employees among each of the eight language groups. We used these employees to deliver our key messages in the native language for each group.

I learned a lot about layoff communication that day, and I also learned that rather than always reinventing the wheel, having a communication plan library can save a lot of time. It wasn't too hard after that experience to convince me that taking the time to develop other tools and processes also could save time and facilitate continuous improvement.

Following is a look at some common tools most employee communicators will find invaluable in carrying out their daily work.

## Making Organizational Calendars

Perhaps the single most important planning tool employee communicators can have is an up-to-date calendar of events for their organizations. A calendar is necessary for strategic planning and crucial for getting the timing of messages in sync with the organization. An organizational calendar should answer questions such as these:

- When does the fiscal quarter and fiscal year end?
- When are internal budgets approved?
- When are the major software upgrades and the rollout of new software occurring?
- When are major organizational wide initiatives scheduled?
- When do collective bargaining contracts expire?
- What are the major cyclical events that affect the business?
- When are the company holidays?
- When is the company picnic and when are the other major employee events?

A calendar can help ensure that the release of various communications by various departments is coordinated. Timing is often a key element in maximizing effective communication. Sometimes when you say something is just as important as what you say. Imagine if the United Way committee launches its fundraising campaign on the same day the HR department announces pay cuts. Another common problem organizations face is disseminating too many communications at the same time, which dilutes the effectiveness of each one. By scheduling the communications in a coordinated fashion, communicators can enhance the effectiveness of each communication.

You should meet regularly with your internal clients to find out what important activities each department has planned. You also may want to create an online calendar that can be updated by individuals throughout your organization. It is common for departments to be unaware of all the activities planned by one another.

In your role as an employee communicator, you partner with nearly every other department in the organization and that makes you well-positioned to be the keeper of a comprehensive centralized calendar. By posting such a calendar online, you can better facilitate your own strategic planning, provide a valuable service for the entire organization and help demonstrate your value to the organization.

# Analyzing Internal Clients

One way to get out in front of your work, and establish yourself as a strategic communicator and executive counselor as described in Chapter 2, is by conducting interviews and a SWOT (strengths, weaknesses, opportunities and threats) analysis with appropriate executives and key internal clients. This common business analysis technique can be easily applied to strategic communications and make you a better business partner.

Figure 3.1 shows a typical SWOT Analysis Matrix and how you can adapt it with your own questions for your own purposes. Asking questions about upcoming priorities will allow you to be more proactive, and getting feedback on how internal communication is perceived is invaluable. You may discover you have an image problem, or you may discover that something you are

**Figure 3.1: Typical SWOT Analysis Matrix and Adaptation**

| | HELPFUL | HARMFUL |
|---|---|---|
| **Attributes of the Organization / Department** | Strengths<br>• What are the strengths of the organization and your department? | Weaknesses<br>• What challenges are the organization and your team facing? |
| **Attributes of the Environment** | Opportunities<br>• What opportunities do you see in the current state or on the horizon? | Threats<br>• Does the current situation pose any potential threats to the organization or to your department? |
| **Attributes of the Department** | Strengths<br>• What are your top priorities right now?<br><br>• What major priorities are on the horizon?<br><br>• What do you wish the rest of the organization knew about your team? | Weaknesses<br>• What challenges being faced by your team are preventing it from being more successful?<br><br>• What areas are you trying to improve within your team? |
| **Attributes of the Environment** | Opportunities<br>• Has the internal communication team been helpful to your team in the past?<br><br>• What do you see as the strengths and the weaknesses of the internal communication team?<br><br>• What do you wish the internal communication team did more of? What do you wish it would do less of?<br><br>• How do you see the internal communication team working with your team going forward?<br><br>• How can the internal communication team be more helpful? | Threats<br>• What outside obstacles are preventing your team from being more successful?<br><br>• Are there changes going on in the industry that are putting additional pressures on your team? |

doing has a greater perceived value to your clients than you realized. You'll never know until you ask.

A good time to conduct such an analysis is at the conclusion of a business cycle such as the conclusion of the fiscal year or a business quarter as the client or executive is preparing for the next cycle to begin.

## Determining Demographics

Another tool you need is a list of demographics for your organization so you can better understand your audiences. Because demographics change over time, you should update the demographic list at least once a year. The responsibility of creating and updating most of the demographics for an organization usually falls upon the HR department. HR departments use Human Resource Information Management Systems such as PeopleSoft or Cyborg to compile employee data. They usually can slice and dice demographic data in any number of ways. It will be up to you to tell them what specific demographic data you want.

Typically, employee communicators want general organizational data such as how many overall employees, how many male and female employees, the average age of employees, the ethnic make-up of the workforce, languages spoken in the workplace and the average length of service. You'll also want audience specific information by job titles, workgroups and work locations. Here are some specific categories that may be helpful for you to have:

- Total employees (listed overall and by individual workgroups)
- Full-time employees
- Part-time employees
- Senior vice presidents
- Vice presidents
- Directors
- Managers
- Corporate office employees
- Frontline employees (listed overall and by location)
- International employees (listed overall and by location)

- Union employees (listed overall and by union)
- Retirees (if there is an active retiree group)

In addition to gathering data from the HR department, you should gather some data from the IT department to find out such things as:

- How many employees have e-mail access?
- Can employees access e-mail from home?
- How many employees have company provided mobile devices?
- What platforms are being used on desktops?
- What is the intranet browser standard?

All this demographic information will help you understand your organization and your audiences better, and will enable you to put together more effective communication plans as a result.

## Making Your Own Communication Style Guide

Consistency in communication is important for achieving maximum success. Consistency helps make messages more powerful and can help drive brand behavior among employees. Language is part of the organization's culture and by changing words employees use, you can begin to change the culture. For example, Disneyland refers to its customers as "guests" and its employees as "cast members" who are part of a show. I did some benchmarking with Disney that included a "backstage" tour, and I can tell you from personal experience that it takes those brand words quite seriously. When I was at PetSmart, we referred to our customers as "pet parents" and the store employees who find solutions for them as "pet detectives." The consistent, long-term and broad use of brand terminology helps drive subtle differences in employee brand behavior.

Having your own written style guide containing rules for word usage is one tool that can help drive consistency throughout your organization. It may sound like a lot of work to create your own style guide. To make it a less daunting task, start by just typing in rules for the top 10 words you use in your organization. Then, add to the document as word situations arise. Within a month or two, you'll have a pretty good guide. Figure 3.2 is a sample style guide designed to help create a partnership tone in an organization. (We'll talk about various tones in more detail in Chapter 6.) Feel free to use or adapt anything you'd like from my sample style guide to jump-start your own.

Most communicators are familiar with, and in many cases devoted to, *The Associated Press Stylebook*. Keep in mind that AP Style was created specifically for newspapers, so it doesn't include many of the industry terms and phrases unique to an organization's daily needs. For instance, retail companies use a host of words pertaining to their in-store displays and signage including end-caps, power-wings, bump-outs and plan-o-grams. AP simply doesn't cover such industry terminology.

AP Style may serve as a good starting point, but I advise organizations to develop their own style guides as a supplement. You can share the guide with your communication partners throughout your organization to help drive consistency. Or, if you subscribe to *The Associated Press Stylebook* online (www.apstylebook.com), it allows you to add your own custom entries and notes to AP listings.

**Figure 3.2: Sample Style Guide**

Our company seeks to establish a partnership tone when communicating with our employees. This style guide is a step toward that objective.

**about** and **approximately** The less stilted and shorter "about" is preferred.

**acronyms** Do not use a period between letters. (e.g., FBI, not F.B.I.). Should be spelled out on first reference unless very well known (such as FBI). In general, acronyms that are said as words, rather than individual letters, should be upper-/lowercase (e.g., "Zip" code but "IBM").

**affect** The verb meaning to influence. Do not confuse with "effect," a noun.

**appositives** Commas must be used to separate appositions. These are clauses that provide additional clarification to the subject expressed just before them, but are not necessary to making the sentence complete. Examples: "His wife, Jane, said ..." "The event will be held Dec. 1, 2014, in the multipurpose room ..." "XYZ Corp. has been headquartered in Nebraska City, Neb., since 1983." "Smith, 44, is in charge of the program."

**audiotape**, not "audio-tape" or "audio tape."

**because**, instead of "due to" or "since."

**before**, preferred over "prior to."

**between** and **among** Use "between" when comparing two things. Use "among" when comparing three or more things.

**bullets**, punctuation of Commas should not be used to separate bulleted items. A period should be used on bulleted items if they are complete sentences. A period should be used at the end of a simple series.

### Correct Example:
The list includes the following:
- Red
- Blue
- Black.

### Incorrect Example:
The list includes the following:
- red,
- blue and
- black

**capitalization** In general, avoid unnecessary capitalization. Capitalize proper names and proper nouns. Do not capitalize shortened titles (such as company, committee, department, federal) unless they are one-of-a-kind events (such as the Kentucky Derby).

**CEO** Well known enough to abbreviate on first reference.

**collective nouns** Remember that collective nouns require singular verbs. Examples: "The family is …" but "The sisters are …" or "The team is …" but "The players are …" Exception to the Rule: If the members of a group are acting separately, or disagree, the collective noun takes a plural verb (e.g., the jury have failed to meet on a verdict). It is clearer to write around such awkward sentences by including a phrase such as "the members of" (e.g., the members of the jury have failed to reach a verdict).

**company** Contrary to AP style, "Company" is not abbreviated as "Co." Consistent with AP Style, "company" should be lowercase in all instances unless part of a formal title or at the beginning of a sentence. This differs from a style preferred in many legal instruments and contracts.

**compliment**, means to express praise and should not be confused with "complement" meaning something that adds, makes whole or brings to perfection.

**contractions**, are preferred to help achieve the conversational tone of our brand.

**country**, use "nation" instead.

**dates** should be abbreviated. Example: "The event will be held Jan. 1." However, a month used without a date should be spelled out. Example: "The event will be held in January." Do not include the ordinal, such as "November 11th" or "Nov. 11th."

**department**, use "team" instead.

**departments** Formal department titles should be capitalized, but not the word "department," unless it is part of the formal name. However, "team" is favored over "department" in most cases.

**effect** The noun that is often confused with "affect," a verb.

**ellipses** (...), indicate missing words in a sentence. They do not indicate pauses in speaking and should not be used in place of a comma, a long dash, etc.

**e-mail,** not "email" or "E-mail" (capitalize only if it is the first word in a sentence).

**exclamation marks** Be careful not to overuse! Using them on things that really aren't that exciting dilutes other messages and makes your copy less credible. Multiple marks probably won't have the effect you intend. Rather than excitement, most readers likely will regard them as amateurish and will be more skeptical of your claims.

**e.g.** To avoid sounding technical, use "for example" instead.

**ensure** Preferred over "insure," unless referring to liability insurance.

**fax**, not FAX. It is not an acronym. It is short for "facsimile."

**401(k)**, not "401(K)" or "401K." Refers to a specific section of the Internal Revenue Code that allows for tax-deferred employee investments.

**frontline**, not "front-line." Do not refer to the frontline as being "down" as in "communicate down to the frontline."

**hotline** not "hot-line" or "hot line." Capitalize if part of formal name.

**hyphenation** In general, prefixes are not hyphenated unless two vowels would otherwise be connected. Exceptions include reengineering and reelection.

**hyphenation of modifiers and compound nouns.** Modifiers and compound nouns should be hyphenated to avoid confusion as to which word is being modified. Example: "Small appliance store" compared to "Small-appliance store." The first phrase refers to a small store that sells appliances. The second phrase refers to a store that sells small appliances. The hyphen shows the reader that "small" is referring to "appliance" and not store. Note: adverbs ending in "ly" are never hyphenated unless they do not form a word with the suffix removed, such as "early."

**i.e.** To avoid sounding too technical, use "such as" instead.

**"in order to"** and **"in order for,"** use "to" and "for" instead.

**insure** Ensure is preferred, unless referring to liability insurance.

**media**, to avoid confusion, specify "News Media" or "Advertising Media."

**man (as a verb)** Avoid the sexist language and use "staff" or "work" instead. Examples: "Jane will staff the booth and the trade show." "The project will require 50 staff hours."

**millions, billions** Per AP style, express as numerals even when less than 10 (For example, 3 billion).

**more than** Means in excess of and is generally preferred in place of "over." Over is best left for sentences such as "She flew over the city in a helicopter."

**nation**, preferred over "country" but use company-wide when it makes sense to do so because it includes our international locations.

**numbers** Amounts in single digits are spelled out and double digits written numerically. However, many figures expressed as quantities are written numerically even when they are a single digit. This includes ages, percentages, gallons, pints, quarts, acres, feet, inches.

**OK**, not "okay" or "O.K."

**online**, not "on-line."

**parenthesis periods** Periods go inside of parenthesis if the words inside the parenthesis form a complete sentence. They go outside of the parenthesis if part of a sentence.

**percent** Contrary to AP Style, use the "%" sign. Also, percentages always are expressed as numerals, even when less than 10 (e.g. 3 percent).

**phone numbers** Contrary to AP style, 800 and 888 numbers will be written as 1-800 and 1-888 because no matter where you are calling from, you must use a 1. Other area codes will be written as 602/444-4444 to facilitate parenthesis.

**prior to**, "before" is preferred.

**Realtor** Use "real estate agent" unless you mean the person is a member of the National Association of Realtors.

**reenginering**, not "re-engineering," according to Michael Hammer who coined the term. This also avoids the problem of "pre-re-engineering" and "post-re-engineering."

**regard**, not "regards."

**said**, not "says," unless it is an ongoing thought such as "The sign says no smoking" or "The president says he is against increasing taxation."

**should** Use "if" instead when it makes sense to do so.

**since** Use "because" instead when it makes sense to do so.

**spacing after punctuation** It may not be what you learned in typing class, but since the inception of scalable type, virtually all professional publications use only single spaces after punctuation (periods, colons, exclamation marks and question marks). This is true for newspapers and magazines and online publications. Single spacing allows the software's automatic hyphenation and kerning programs to display your type more attractively.

**state abbreviations** Use AP style abbreviations rather than postal abbreviations unless writing a full address. Postal abbreviations were invented solely for the purpose of an optical character recognition program. Correct Examples: "XYZ Corp. has been headquartered in Nebraska City, Neb, since 1983." "Send the coupon to XYZ Corp. 222 E. Thomas Road, Mainstreet, HI 96709."

**Styrofoam** Use terms like "plastic foam cup" or "insulated cup" unless you mean the specific brand name.

**team**, preferred over "department."

**that and which** "That" is used for an essential clause and "which" is used for nonessential clauses. If a comma is not placed before "which" in a clause, it is not an essential clause. A test is if the sentence could not be deleted from the word "which" on, it is not an essential clause. Correct Example: "These are clauses that provide additional clarification." Incorrect Example: "These are clauses which provide additional clarification."

**through**, preferred over "via."

**time** Use a.m. and p.m. Don't use colons with hours and no minutes. Noon is preferred over 12 p.m. Don't use "o'clock." Correct Example: 1 p.m. Incorrect Example: 1:00 pm.

**titles** Contrary to AP style, complete formal job titles should be capitalized in all instances.

**toward**, not "towards."

**underway**, not "under way." Note that AP recently changed it from two words to one.

**upon**, use "on" instead.

**utilize**, the less stilted and shorter "use" is preferred.

**via**, the less formal "through" is preferred.

**videotape**, not "video-tape" or "video tape."

**voicemail**, not "voice mail."

**website**, not "web site," "Web site" or "Website." Refers to any collection of HTML pages that are accessed through an intranet, an extranet or the internet. This is contrary to AP style.

**which** (see "that")

**whether** or **not**, use "whether"

**workforce** Contrary to AP style, use as one word.

**workplace**, not "work place."

**Xerox** Don't use as a verb and don't use unless referring to the specific brand. Use "photocopy" or "duplicate" instead.

# The AP Stylebook Isn't 'the Bible'

Some employee communicators are so committed to AP style that they will risk their jobs by arguing an AP style rule with their CEOs. I understand this mentality. My father was an old newspaperman, and when I was in college, he used to edit my letters in AP style and send them back to me. But trust me, lowercasing a job title isn't worth jeopardizing your career. Need more convincing? Note this: many AP Style rules were designed not for grammatical reasons but for word hyphenation in narrow newspaper columns and for technical reasons. For instance, AP calls for lowercasing job titles (e.g., "vice president" instead of "Vice President") but many senior officers and other employees in organizations want their titles capitalized and see the lowercasing as a sign of disrespect.

The reasons why AP calls for lowercasing titles are not rooted in anything grammatical. The reason is in fact a holdover from the days when typesetting was done on Linotype machines where uppercasing was a tedious procedure. I spent many hours in my childhood in the back shop of my father's newspaper and saw this firsthand. There is no reason a modern organization should be bound by an archaic rule contained in a manual designed specifically for newspapers.

Here's the bottom line: It is OK for an organization's style guide to contradict AP Style as long as the deviation is:

(1) well thought out

(2) applied consistently.

Communicators should think carefully about all of the applications of a proposed change before implementing it and, once the change is adopted, they must make certain it is carried out consistently across all communications. Need even more convincing? Consider this: Even newspapers sometimes deviate from AP Style when it makes sense to do so. For example, *The Wall Street Journal* uses a percentage sign (%) instead of spelling out the word "percent." This is probably because the *WSJ* editors long ago knew that the newspaper's audience includes a lot of people in the financial industry who are accustomed to seeing the percentage sign rather than the word spelled out. And while we are on the subject of "percent," at one point in history, it was two words (per cent) according to AP Style, just like "per diem" and "per annum" are today. *The Associated Press Stylebook* issues updates from time to time so even AP doesn't see its rules as written in stone.

# Building a Glossary of Terms

A close cousin of the style guide is a Glossary of Terms. A glossary is another tool that can help drive consistency throughout your organization by listing and defining industry and organization terms. Again as an employee communicator who deals with all the others departments in the organization, you are well-positioned to create a glossary for the organization.

Here's an idea you might want to try: Create an online glossary as a wiki and allow designated content experts throughout the organization to maintain and update it. This helps the tool to be even more valuable to the organization, and it helps to engage content experts in the internal communication process. In addition, a glossary is sometimes an effective way to introduce user-generated content to an organization that may be apprehensive about such content. More information about wikis and other communication channels is included in Chapter 4.

# Making Branding Guidelines

Whereas style guides and glossaries can help achieve consistency of words, branding guidelines can help achieve consistency of the look and feel of communication materials. Branding guidelines typically specify what typefaces and colors can be used to be consistent with the corporate brand, and they may include rules detailing how the organization's logo can be used. Branding guidelines are often created by an organization's marketing team and intended primarily for advertising and other external communication.

Ideally, all of an organization's communications, whether they are produced for external or internal audiences, should have a consistent branded look and feel. Employee communicators should adhere to branding guidelines for all internal communication they produce, including e-letters, brochures, posters and intranet sites. You can further promulgate the branded look throughout the organization by providing templates for things like PowerPoint presentations and memos. You also should share the branded style guide with vendors to ensure a further consistent look and feel. For example, most organizations have an outside vendor that administers its healthcare plan. That vendor typically produces communication materials that are sent to employees. By providing the vendor with branding guidelines, the healthcare plan administrator might be willing to change the colors on the communication materials to match the organization's branded colors. In addition, the organization's employee communicators may be able to suggest some minor edits to the healthcare text that could bring it into better alignment with other organizational messaging.

## Formulating Communication Plan Templates

One of the most important things an internal communication professional does is create written communication plans. Clear writing is a reflection of clear thinking. Systematically going through the steps of a communication plan template helps to ensure important elements aren't overlooked. Involving key stakeholders in the planning process will make a better plan, enhance mutual understanding and increase buy-in.

Sometimes the communication planning process itself is the brainstorm catalyst that results in the most creative approaches. A step-by-step process to formulate the communication plan is included in Chapter 5.

Plan the work and then work the plan. Evaluate how successful the plan was and recommend ways it could have been done better. As I mentioned at the beginning of this chapter, keeping a library of completed communication plans can help speed the process of writing a similar plan in the future and facilitate continuous improvement. There are many advantages to having an old plan at your fingertips: Maybe the people who created the plan thought of something you'd forgotten. Maybe something in the old plan sparks your imagination for something you could include in your new plan. Improve upon the old plan and make yours even better. And know that your new plan likely will help someone, maybe even yourself, in the future.

## Creating a Communication Channel Matrix

You will need to understand thoroughly all the communication channels in your organization and determine how each channel matches up with the messages you are communicating and your intended audiences.

Specifically, you need to know:

- What are the strategic purposes of each channel?
- Which channels reach which audiences?
- What are the strengths and weaknesses of each channel?
- When should you use and when should you not use each channel?
- How does each channel integrate with the other channels?

Once the information about each channel is gathered, it may be helpful to include it in a matrix so it can be easily referenced when formulating communication strategies. This concept and samples of communication channel matrixes are included in Chapter 4 in much greater detail.

## Making Templates to Sell the Plan

Once you create a written communication plan, you likely will have to get buy-in from other stakeholders, which could include your boss, senior leadership and internal clients. Some senior leaders and internal clients will simply want to read the written communication plan. Others, however, may find the written communication plan too cumbersome. They may prefer a shorter version of the plan in a format more suited to a tabletop conversation about the plan. One tool that facilitates that purpose is the 4-square template.

As shown in Figure 3.3, the 4-square template is a one-page tool that allows for four key areas of the communication plan to be included. Typically, the 4-square is printed out in a horizontal format on an 8.5 x 11 piece of paper. The four elements can be changed out to suit the plan's needs, but they likely will include a brief situation analysis, goals, tactics and a timeline. When presenting the plan to an internal client, one approach is to use the 4-square template as a visual aid while discussing the plan and then to leave the entire written communication with the client to read at his or her leisure.

The 4-square is just one approach to help get understanding and buy-in for a plan. You'll need to try various approaches with various clients. For example, IT clients often prefer flowcharts to enhance their understanding and will want to know how the plan affects systems whereas finance department clients prefer Excel spreadsheets and likely will be most interested in the cost analysis.

**Figure 3.3: Sample 4-square**

| XYZ Company – Project Name: Town Hall Revamp | |
|---|---|
| **Situation Analysis:**<br>• Employee attendance at the Quarterly Town Hall has declined 20% over the past year.<br>• Q&A questions have declined from an average of 10 to 2 per meeting.<br>• Employee feedback indicates the information presented is too complex and not relevant | **Goals:**<br>• Boost employee attendance by 20%<br>• Increase the number of Q&A questions to 10.<br>• Simplify content and ensure it is relevant. |
| **Strategies:**<br>• Create an internal marketing plan that includes e-mail invites, break room table tents, digital signage and intranet banner ads.<br>• Revise meeting format to allow for more interaction.<br>• Convey complet information using interactive scenarios and graphics.<br>• Involve employees in content creation and meeting planning. | **Timeline:**<br>• Form employee committee and present content recommendations by 2/11.<br>• Develop and launch marketing plan by 2/15.<br>• Finalize meeting format and present to Senior Team by 3/1<br>• Relaunch Town Hall 4/7. |

# Using Surveys and Feedback Mechanisms

You should collect as much data as you can that provides insights about employee engagement and your audiences. Some of the questions you'll want answers to include:

• How well do employees understand the mission and vision of your organization?

• How do they want to receive information about the organization?

• Do employees believe the organization is transparent enough?

• Are the organization's leaders credible?

• Are employees committed to the organization's success?

In many organizations, the HR team conducts engagement surveys. You should obtain data from past surveys and offer to partner with HR on future surveys. You may want to conduct your own communication surveys and focus groups, and create feedback mechanisms to ascertain the effectiveness of your communications. Once you collect survey data and feedback, you'll want to find appropriate ways to share the evidence with executives and your key internal clients. Chapter 10 details evaluation techniques and how to share results.

## Formulating Budgets

Whoever is leading the internal communication team will need to become familiar with the organization's budgeting process, including capital expense requirements, appropriate charge codes and the budget approval process.

Budgets are typically set annually. If the employee communicators have proposed expenses for the coming year, they need to have buy-in from their leaders and clients in time for the budget approval process. Ideally, the process would work in the following manner: The employee communicators would meet to draft a strategic plan for the following year. In that plan, they would identify any items that would need to be paid for from their annual budget. They then would have to get an estimate of what those items cost. The next step would be to get buy-in from any affected partners on the proposed expenses. For instance, if the expense were for enhancements to the intranet, the leaders of the employee communicators may need to have the support of their counterparts in IT. Finally, with estimates and buy-in in hand, the communicators would put forth their proposed budget in time for the budget review process. I also recommend you request some funding in an ad hoc budget bucket to handle unplanned projects that emerge from time to time. The entire process can take time. It is not uncommon for the communicators to start their planning process in March of one year for a budget that will go into effect in January the following year.

In addition to understanding your own budget, it will serve you well to understand how your business operates financially. Finance is the language of business and you must learn to speak it if you are going to be taken seriously. Know and understand:

• What the key drivers of your business are

• What are the business strategies unique to your organization

• What are the key economic indicators that affect your organization.

## Using Project Request Forms

Having a written project request form that captures key information may help you better manage the inflow of your work. Maybe it's a news submission form that's on the intranet and part of an automated workflow process, or maybe it's a paper form a client completes about his project before you meet with him personally. Take a close look at how incoming work gets to you and look for opportunities to collect information more efficiently. Forms also can provide an opportunity to explain internal communication policies to your clients.

> Having well-established communication tools and processes will help you to be on time, on budget and on brand.

## Creating Checklists

Written checklists are a good way to help ensure high-quality work, consistency and business continuity. Don't underestimate the power of simple checklists. Putting the time and effort into creating them will help ensure important steps aren't missed. Using them consistently will help eliminate mistakes, and having them in writing allows them to be transferred to someone else who may be filling in or new on the job.

For example, you might want to create a checklist to be used before sending out a company-wide e-mail. No matter how many times I've done it, I always worry when I hit the send button. Nothing is worse than having to resend a company-wide e-mail because of a mistake. As communicators, we're naturally detail-oriented people. But we often find ourselves sending out company-wide messages at the end of a long day when we're tired and in a rush. Having a checklist makes the process a little less worrisome.

Here's what I've included on my e-mail checklist:

- Make sure the distribution list is correct.
- Make sure the subject field is complete and all words are spelled correctly.

- Make sure all telephone numbers contained in the message are correct (double-check them by actually calling the numbers).

- Make sure all hyperlinks are working properly.

## Formulating Guiding Principles

You should create a written list of the communication principles that guide your daily decisions and help you in your long-term strategic communication planning. Once completed, you can share your principles with key stakeholders, including your organization's senior leaders, to help them understand more about the philosophies that drive effective internal communication strategies.

A list of some guiding principles I've used over the years to guide me along a path to maximizing internal communication and fully engaging employees is contained in the back of this book. You'll find references to each of my guiding principles woven throughout this book. I've found these guiding principles to be powerful ideas, and understanding them fully and applying them consistently can change your professional life.

## Chapter Conclusion

Having well-established communication tools and well-defined communication processes gives the internal communication function a solid foundation upon which to build great communication programs. They help you to be on time, on budget and on brand. Rather than being time-consuming and confining, the "tools and rules" approach can help make you and your team run like a well-oiled machine and can be a springboard to breakthrough thinking.

You'll have to adapt tools to suit your own need. The important thing is that you begin to create and use them so you can plan your work, and not have the work control you. Only then can you position yourself as a strategic communicator and as an executive counselor.

## Chapter Exercises

1. What is the single most useful tool for an employee communicator?

_____

2. What two criteria must be present to contradict AP style in internal communication?

_____

_____

3. Explain how a style guide can help drive brand behavior in an organization.

_____

_____

_____

_____

_____

_____

# Chapter 4

# Choosing the Right Channels

"I talked to a calzone for 15 minutes last night before I realized it was just an introverted pizza."
– Jarod Kintz

**Chapter Overview:** The most carefully crafted messages can fall flat if they aren't communicated via the right channel. In this chapter, you'll learn how to use a strategic communication channel matrix to help you know which channel to use to reach which audience for what purpose. Understanding the strategic purpose, the strengths and weaknesses and when to use and not to use each communication channel is one of the necessary steps in becoming a strategic communicator and another crucial step to maximizing internal communication.

M any channels are available to employee communicators today and new ones are emerging all the time. There are new channels such as video blogs, interactive webcasts, podcasts, wikis, e-letters, internal social media platforms and digital signage. There are tried and true channels such as newsletters, posters, brochures, memos, table tents and good old face-to-face communication. Leaders of organizations count on their internal communication professionals to determine the most effective communication channels to reach their employees.

To determine which channels to use for a specific communication, internal communication professionals typically answer these four questions:

- Who is the audience we are trying to reach?
- Which channels reach that audience?
- What is the outcome we are seeking?
- Which channels work best to achieve that outcome?

Answering these questions requires identification of each employee audience, an inventory of the channels that reach each audience, an understanding of the communication goals, and a thorough analysis of the capabilities of each channel.

## Using an Internal Communication Channel Matrix

Aligning the various employee audiences, the channels that reach them, the communication goals and the capabilities of each channel is necessary to achieve maximum effectiveness, but that can be an overwhelming exercise without some methodology to help organize it. One thing that can help you to make effective channel choices is to create a communication channel matrix, such as the one shown in Figure 4.1. Once all the information is included in the matrix, it can be easily referenced when formulating communication strategies and it can be shared with internal clients and your management team to help them understand the rationale behind the choice.

The information in Figure 4.1 shows three communication channels the fictitious internal communication professionals at XYZ Corporation are considering adding to their mix. They already have a weekly hardcopy newsletter, a daily e-letter, an intranet and corporate e-mail, but they are looking for ways to drive deeper understanding and more fully engage their employees. Take a look at how the matrix helps to organize the information about each channel in a digestible format.

Each section of the communication matrix contains important information that can guide decision-making about which communication channels to use. You likely will find that the thought process you go through to create each of those sections is quite illuminating and where the true value of the matrix lies. Let's look at each section and the thinking behind it.

## Identifying Channels

You should create a comprehensive list of all the communication channels available in your organization. These will, of course, include the formal channels you oversee, such as newsletters, e-letters, intranets, webcasts, videos, podcasts, digital signage, etc. The CEO and other organizational

## Figure 4.1: Communication Channel Matrix

### XYZ CORPORATION COMMUNICATION CHANNEL MATRIX

| CHANNELS | WIKI | PODCAST | SENIOR LEADER BLOGS |
|---|---|---|---|
| **Strategic Purpose** | • To facilitate collaboration, brainstorming and information sharing, and help to engage employees by having them participate in the process. | • To communicate a complex set of messages or issues in a digestible format. | • To allow direct and regularly updated communication from leaders in a way that's personal and inspirational to their individual team members. |
| **Audiences** | • All Corporate Office<br>• Field Management<br>• Frontline Employees<br>• Sales Associates | • All Corporate Office<br>• Field Management<br>• Frontline Employees (Note: some do not have sound cards.)<br>• Sales Associates | • Management and employees of each specific work team. |
| **Advantages** | • Engages content experts.<br>• Shares knowledge across a broad audience.<br>• Easy to use collaboration software.<br>• Can be linked from e-letter, e-mail and intranet.<br>• Can be searched with intranet. | • Audio is more personal and more emotional than print.<br>• Can use with RSS to push to subscribers.<br>• Portable – Can be downloaded to smartphones.<br>• Can be archived in a topical library.<br>• Can be linked to from e-letter, e-mail and intranet. | • Connects leaders in a personal way with their employees who previously had little or no contact with<br>• Creates trust through ongoing conversation.<br>• Positions leaders as thought leaders.<br>• Can use with RSS to push to subscribers.<br>• Can track readership.<br>• Can incorporate photos, videos, polls, and discussion topics.<br>• Can be linked to from intranet and e-mails. |
| **Disadvantages** | • Limited purpose.<br>• Edits need to be monitored by content experts. | • Can't have live participation or real time feedback.<br>• Can't reach employees without sound cards.<br>• Sound editing tool requires some training. | • May be too tedious to read a long message.<br>• May be difficult to keep producing fresh content. |
| **When to Use** | • To document team processes and Best Practice.<br>• To create glossaries, style guides, collaborative storytelling, Policies & Procedures and other reference documents that need to be updated routinely by a wide variety of associates.<br>• For input from a lot of people. | • For content experts to drive deeper understanding of complex topics.<br>• For hot topics.<br>• To answer recurring questions.<br>• With small expert panel discussions.<br>• To humanize a subject.<br>• When sounds can enhance a message (music, sound effects).<br>• For leaders who prefer talking over writing and who can speak well without a script. | • To deliver timely and candid info on trends and issues.<br>• For personal storytelling.<br>• To share best practices.<br>• To create a genuine dialogue.<br>• To connect leaders to employees and build community, particularly when audience is dispersed throughout the field.<br>• When leader is a natural communicator and has relevant information to say to his team. |
| **When Not to Use** | • If an expert can't monitor content.<br>• For one-to-many communication. | • With a lot of facts and figures that need to be remembered (unless supplemented by written text).<br>• When can't be condensed into a 10-minute timeframe.<br>• With content experts who aren't dynamic speakers. | • If leader isn't going to write him- or herself.<br>• When purpose isn't clear.<br>• If the leader can't update frequently.<br>• When there isn't relevant information to convey.<br>• If the messages should be more formal. |
| **Works Well With** | • Links from other intranet sites.<br>• Policies and Procedures.<br>• Group brainstorms.<br>• Project teams. | • Topical libraries.<br>• E-letters. | • Online instant polls.<br>• Feedback boards.<br>• Relevant photos and video clips. |

leaders also might be considered official communication channels because they could be called upon to make speeches, lead large-scale meetings, write blogs, etc. All formal communication channels should be listed on the communication matrix so they can be analyzed further.

You also should be aware of all formal channels over which you don't have direct control, such as union publications and websites, business spreadsheet reports, and departmental staff meetings, newsletters, websites and bulletin boards. You should visit various work areas within your organization to observe and ask where employees in that area go to obtain the information they need to get their jobs done. The answers can be enlightening as to how communication actually occurs as opposed to how management perceives it is occurring. Often a query will uncover new channels you weren't aware of and the line manager of that work area didn't report. It is not that the line manager is trying to hide anything; it is just that line managers and most other employees don't think of communication channels in the same manner we internal communication professionals do.

Finally, you should be aware of informal communication channels including influential employees who aren't in official leadership positions, the ubiquitous rumor mill and the organization's culture itself, which is exemplified by its policies and actions. It is important to ascertain whether the organization's "do" matches its "say." For example, if the organization says customer service is the most important thing it does, then its policies toward customers, its budget for customer service initiatives, its staffing levels for customer service representatives and so on should be in alignment with the stated customer service value. Otherwise, this informal organizational culture channel undermines the formal channels.

## Understanding the Strategic Purpose

It is important that you understand the strategic purpose of each communication channel. Listing them in the matrix will help remind everyone involved in the planning process of each communication channel's purpose, and it will help to identify which channels work best for which particular outcomes you are trying to achieve. The outcome is what the communicators want the audience to do, to think or to feel as a result of receiving the message being sent.

Strategies should drive tactics, not the other way around. Communicators can't consistently achieve maximum effectiveness if the tactics are driving the strategies. For example, if it is to achieve maximum effectiveness, an organization shouldn't have a "social media strategy." Instead, it should have a communication strategy that might include the use of various social media channels. Internally, that strategy might be to engage employees because engagement is clearly one of social media's strengths. But by focusing on the strategy and not the particular tactic, other tactics that engage employees might also come to mind. Those additional tactics could include holding town hall style meetings, enabling employees to comment on on-line news articles and asking employees to submit worksite photos to be used as a Photo of the Day on the organization's intranet home page. These additional tactics working with internal social media channels make a powerful combination. Social media channels typically don't replace traditional channels; they augment them.

When strategy drives communication planning, more creative tactics are produced and better results are achieved. We'll discuss strategies and tactics, and how they fit into an overall strategic communication plan, in much greater detail in Chapter 5, Strategic Communication Planning.

A communication channel can get information out, but it takes a well-executed communication strategy involving multiple communication channels to get information through to employees in a consistent manner. In order for communication to be effective, some sort of behavior or belief change must occur and that requires multiple channels working together over a period of time. Two reasons exist for this requirement:

1. **Individuals differ on how they process information.**
   Some people process better with tactile methods, such as hands-on learning. Others process information better by hearing or seeing. In my experience, a communication plan that uses multiple channels has a better chance at reaching all the employees than one that employs a single channel.

2. **A multi-channel approach is more effective because of how we are moved to change.**
   In general, logic causes us to think but emotion causes us to act (Weiss, 2002). We need to win both heads and hearts to affect change. Some communication channels lend themselves well to making the logical case (i.e., charts and graphs) and some are better at appealing to emotions (i.e., photographs).

## Identifying Audiences

You need to understand thoroughly the various employee audiences present in your organization. As discussed in Chapter 3, you should obtain audience demographics and continuously look for ways to deepen your understanding of these audiences through surveys, focus groups and anecdotal feedback. You need to identify all potential audiences. For the communication channel matrix' purposes, you need to know which communication channels reach which employee audiences. You need to know the answers to questions such as: Which employees have e-mail and intranet access? Can employees access the e-mail system and the intranet from home? Has the intranet been optimized for mobile devices? What do the tracking analytics suggest about actual e-mail engagement and intranet usage? Which employees have a company mailbox? Which employees have company smartphones? Can employees access the company intranet from their personal mobile devices?

It also might be helpful for you to know which communication channels each audience prefers, but that is only one clue to which channel you might end up using for any given communication. Relying solely on audience preference may not produce the best result. The audience members may not know all the channels available. They can't evaluate channels that haven't been introduced yet. Their preference might be a general response that isn't valid under particular circumstances. For example, employees across all industries consistently list their direct supervisor as their preferred source of information. That's in part because the supervisor can put the information into context for the employees and make the information relevant for their specific work team. But that might not hold true for information about employee benefits because the direct supervisor probably isn't considered an expert on that subject.

## Understanding Advantages and Disadvantages

Each communication channel has inherent strengths and weaknesses. For example, video is a highly effective medium to evoke strong emotions from most people, but it is not a particularly effective medium to convey a long list of complex step-by-step instructions that need to be remembered. By contrast, it can be difficult to evoke strong emotions with printed materials, but printed materials can be highly effective at conveying complex information, such as step-by-step instructions.

Imagine a safety video shown to linemen at an electric utility that features an interview with the widow of an employee who was electrocuted to death in a tragic accident because he failed to follow the proper steps to repair a downed high-voltage power line. In the video, the widow talks about how her husband isn't there for her and their four children. She says she loves him and wishes he had followed procedures so he would still be alive today. Her words are subtly enhanced with dramatic lighting and music. The video presents a powerful message, and it wouldn't be surprising if some audience members had to wipe tears away as the widow spoke. It is doubtful the same story told in a printed newsletter would have as dramatic an impact. The printed piece wouldn't show the widow's distraught face. Readers couldn't hear the sadness in her voice. The printed article wouldn't have dramatic lighting and music to help set the mood.

But now it is time to provide the linemen with a reminder of the step-by-step instructions needed to repair downed power lines safely. The step-by-step instructions need to be carried out flawlessly and referred to on the job. A video format won't be nearly as effective as a printed piece for this purpose.

The internal communication professionals in this example decide the video should be shown during a safety meeting, and then the step-by-step instructions are distributed to the linemen on laminated cards at the meeting's conclusion. Simple colorful pictures are used with the text to illustrate exactly how the procedure is to be performed. The linemen are able to carry the cards into the field and the lamination adds durability and protection from dirt and grime.

The internal communication professionals are able to leverage each communication channel for what it does best. Their communication plan allows the two channels to work together and complement one another. They recognize that a multi-channel approach is needed to deliver the complete message and achieve the maximum effect. They probably will suggest additional communications to serve as reminders.

Existing communication channels should be evaluated from time to time to ensure their strengths are being leveraged and their weaknesses avoided.

Figure 4.2 shows an analysis of the fictitious XYZ Corporation's use of printed materials and Figure 4.3 shows a proposal to bring its monthly hardcopy newsletter, *Inside XYZ*, into alignment with print's inherent strengths and weaknesses. XYZ Corporation wants to continue some form of printed communication because a significant portion of its workforce doesn't have computer access.

## Figure 4.2: Print Analysis

Some printed information is outdated before it comes off the printing press, and it can be costly to produce and distribute. But while there are much faster and less expensive ways to communicate to employees, a place for print may still exist at XZY Corporation.

   Here are some situations when XYZ Corporation should consider using print:

- When the information needs to be portable, such as employee benefits materials that need to be taken home and shared with a spouse. (Note: as mobile devices become increasingly more prevalent, print's portability advantage will become lessened.)
- When the information is complex, contains a lot of facts and figures and requires time for study.
- When photos, charts, graphs or illustrations need to be high-quality and large.
- When the message needs to look official and important, such as legal documents.
- When a print vehicle such as a news magazine or poster can reach employee audiences that other channels can't reach.
- When speed is not of the essence.

## Figure 4.3: Repurposing Inside XYZ

*Inside XYZ* has been providing employees with news articles and photographs every week for the past 30 years. The publication has good name recognition and is still popular among employees. A significant portion of the XYZ Corporation workforce doesn't have access to a computer so *Inside XYZ* is an important communication channel for these employees. But the news in *Inside XYZ* is often outdated before the ink dries. In addition, the company is going through a difficult financial period and the senior leadership team is looking for ways to cut costs. Some have suggested that the internal communication team should discontinue publishing *Inside XYZ*. However, maybe the publication just needs to be repurposed to do what print does best. As shown in Figure 4.2, print has some advantages over digital communication. There are some easy ways to reduce costs, too.

The XYZ communicators propose transforming the weekly newsletter into a monthly magazine. The new format will leverage the inherent advantages of print in the following ways:

- The newsletter design will be replaced with a magazine look.

- The lengthy and stale news stories and grip-and-grin photos will be replaced with short feature articles and large compelling photos.

- The cover will no longer have a lead news story on it but instead will have a large cover photo and teasers about what's inside.

- The center spread will feature large photos of employees on the job.

- The tone of the writing will change from hard news to lively feature copy with a longer shelf life.

- The magazine will become a channel for the facts and figures the organization wants to communicate to employees. For instance, the company's quarterly financial report could be analyzed and put into context for employees in the magazine. The article could include large, colorful charts and graphs to help employees understand the complex financial issues the company is facing.

The new magazine format will save the company money by cutting production and distribution costs in the following ways:

- The four-page weekly newsletter will be changed to a monthly 16-page magazine. That will be a net page reduction of four pages per month and will save printing costs.

- Instead of being delivered 52 times a year, the *Inside XYZ* will only be delivered 12 times a year.

- The communicators will perform an audit to make sure all copies of the publication are being picked up and will adjust the press run accordingly to reduce printing costs further.

- The communicators will renegotiate the printing contract with the outside vendor who may be willing to reduce printing costs instead of losing the business completely.

- If further cost reductions are needed, the communicators propose publishing the magazine just 10 times a year (eliminating the two busiest months in the business) or every two months or quarterly before eliminating it entirely.

The communicators know that going from 4-color to black and white seldom saves significant amounts of money, but it does often affect management and employee perception. If asked to print the magazine in black and white, the communicators recommend considering a dark blue rather than black. The dark color will still accommodate text and will allow for tint blocks as well. For example, screening the blue at 20% for a box and placing 100% blue type in it will give the appearance of two-colors. Of course, you could do this with black as well for a black and gray color scheme.

## Understanding When to Use and When Not to Use

Knowing when to use a channel, under what conditions and in which situations, and when not to use that channel, is important. Just because you can use a particular channel doesn't mean you always should use that channel. The channel must be appropriate for the type of message it is carrying. The channel itself can influence how the audience perceives the intended message. The medium is the message, or at least part of it. Imagine a message about an upcoming budget cut that urges employees to look for savings everywhere they can. Now imagine that message is contained in a news magazine that includes an ornate design and is printed on thick glossy paper with four-color printing. You should always ask yourself whether the channel is appropriate for the message.

For purposes of the communication matrix, it is helpful to list some specific uses that are good and some situations to avoid. This will further help determine whether the channel will help achieve the desired outcome.

## Identifying What Works Well With What

Internal communication is more effective when the channels are all leveraging their inherent strengths and when they are coordinated with one another. A short news article on the intranet links to a podcast for more details, a video is shown, and then a handout is given out with information to be taken home and so on.

You should take time to analyze all the formal communication channels in your organization to see whether those channels are coordinated with one another to create a synergy. The channels should cross-reference each other. The channels should be updated in a coordinated fashion and in conjunction with the business cycle. For example, many organizations have a leadership meeting. The individual leaders at that meeting also have their own departmental meetings. And the managers who attend the departmental leader's meetings often have their own staff meetings. But often, no thought has been given to aligning all of those meetings so messages can cascade from one meeting to the next and so feedback can flow up. By simply coordinating the timing of the meetings, a more powerful communication channel can be created.

> The channel must be appropriate for the type of message it is carrying.

For purposes of the communication channel matrix, internal communication professionals should briefly list what areas each channel works well with to help stimulate thought during strategic communication planning.

## Chapter Conclusion

We began the chapter by suggesting that the answers to four questions were needed to ascertain which communication channels to use. Let's look again at these four questions and put them in the context of the communication matrix:

- Who is the audience you are trying to reach? This is answered with our knowledge of our audiences and in the brief description in the audience section of the matrix.

- Which channels reach that audience? This is answered in our knowledge of the formal and informal channels and our brief description of them in the channels section of the matrix.

- What is the outcome you are seeking? This is answered by our determination of specific communication goals and the behavior we are trying to accomplish.

- Which channels work best to achieve that outcome? This is answered by our understanding of each channel's strategic purpose, its strengths and weaknesses, its advantages and disadvantages, and how the channels can work together to create a powerful synergy.

Having a written communication channel matrix can be a good reminder for you of the characteristics of each channel, and it could be a nice visual tool to have when discussing various options with an internal client. But more important than having the physical tool itself is the enlightenment that comes from the strategic and deep thinking that went into creating it. That's the real power of the communication channel matrix.

Choosing the right communication channel is important. But, of course, many other factors can impact the effectiveness of any given communication. Those factors include having the right message for the right audience, the right timing, message credibility, and a way to get feedback and refresh messages as needed. In Chapter 5, we'll explore how to bring all these elements together in a comprehensive strategic communication plan.

### Chapter Exercises
1. List two reasons why an employee communicator might choose a printed piece to communicate a message.

_____

_____

2. Explain what is meant by the phrase "the medium is the message."

_____

_____

_____

_____

_____

_____

# Planning Strategically

"Plans are nothing; planning is everything."
– Dwight D. Eisenhower

**Chapter Overview:** Perhaps the most valued-added activity internal communication professionals perform for their organizations is strategic communication planning. The rigor of the process can help ensure that a project is executed flawlessly and the methodology can help spawn the creative solutions needed to solve an organization's most complex communication problems. In this chapter, you'll learn a step-by-step methodology to create a comprehensive strategic internal communication plan that will give you the best chance at attaining your communication goals and achieving meaningful business results for your organization.

**W**hether an employee communicator is creating a communication plan to support a large-scale initiative or a simple plan to support a small one-off project, the same basic process steps should be followed to achieve a strategic communication plan. As pointed out in Chapter 4, strategies should drive tactics and not the other way around. Following the basic steps shown in Figure 5.1 will help to ensure a strategic outcome and an effective plan.

The final step, Measure Effectiveness, is to determine whether the entire process needs to be refreshed. If the communication were not successful, it could be for a number of reasons. Maybe an important audience was missed. Maybe something else going on in the organization at the same time shifted attention away from the message or caused it to be seen in another light. Maybe the objectives weren't clear. Maybe the messages were misinterpreted or were unclear. Maybe additional communication channels are needed. Or maybe the communication wasn't as successful as it could be because of a combination of these possibilities. Employee communicators need to evaluate the situation and determine how to refresh the process.

The weakest part of most strategic planning efforts is a failure to evaluate effectiveness properly. I have served as a contest judge for IABC and as an exam evaluator for the IABC accreditation process, so I can tell you that measurement is usually what separates the winners from all others. A lot of great communicators do a lot of great work, but it too often goes unrecognized because they do not evaluate their work. You have the opportunity to learn how to evaluate your work's effectiveness, and to share it with your internal clients and your senior leadership team. It is an important step in positioning yourself as a strategic communicator who deserves a seat at the table.

Chapter 10, Evaluating Internal Communication Effectiveness, discusses ways to evaluate message effectiveness, business impact and changes in awareness, depth of understanding, perceptions, attitudes, beliefs, workplace behaviors, commitment and the level of employee engagement. This chapter will discuss evaluation as it relates to the communication planning process itself.

**Figure 5.1: Basic Strategic Communication Process**

| Identify Audience | Assess Climate | Set Clear Objectives | Develop Key Messages | Devise Strategies and Execute Tactics | Evaluate |
|---|---|---|---|---|---|
| Who do we want to reach? | What else is going on? | What do we want employees to do? | What do we want them to know and how do we want them to feel? | What channels should we use and when? | Was the message understood? |

**Refresh**

It is important to understand these basic steps and why they are needed, but additional steps should be considered to achieve the most effective plan possible. The remainder of this chapter presents an approach to creating a comprehensive strategic internal communication plan. This step-by-step approach was first developed in 1997 and honed to perfection over the next 15 years by my colleagues, Lynne Adams Boschee and Bruce Richardson, and me. The methodology has been used in a variety of organizations and industries to create communication plans for virtually every communication situation imaginable, including organizational restructurings, employee lay-offs, leadership changes, mergers, acquisitions, health threats, major production disruptions, large-scale change plans, branding initiatives and company-wide events.

This planning process pre-supposes that you have gathered the necessary tools outlined in Chapter 3 and created a communication channel matrix as outlined in Chapter 4. The entire plan contains the following steps: Title, Date, Project Team, Situational Analysis, Objectives, Goals, Target Audience Analysis, Key Messages, Strategies and Tactics, Action Planning and Timeline, Budget, Evaluation Plan and Project Approval Checklist. Let's look in detail about how employee communicators might approach each section.

## Determining the Title

Writing the title of a plan sounds simple enough, but sometimes a project is so complex that it is difficult to summarize what it is all about in a title. If you're struggling with a title, you might want to create a working title and return to it later. It is important to determine a good title because it will help everyone involved in the planning process to understand the project in simple terms and help communicators to reference the plan years later. As explained in Chapter 2, keeping a library of completed strategic communication plans can help speed the process of writing similar plans and facilitate continuous improvement.

## Writing the Version Date

A date should be included on the title page because several versions of the plan may exist before it is finalized. A date also may help reference the plan in the future.

## Listing the Project Team

It is nearly impossible for you to write a highly effective comprehensive strategic internal communication plan by yourself. No one person can have all the knowledge necessary to produce the best possible plan. For one thing, research will need to be conducted with internal clients and others who will be affected by the plan. Experts from throughout the organization may need to be called upon to contribute to various aspects of the plan. And savvy employee communicators know it is a good practice to get support for their plans early on by including key people in the initial planning process. These communicators know they will be in a much stronger position to get their plans approved if a cross-functional team of experts helped to develop it.

You should consider these questions to determine who should serve on the project team:

- Whom do you need to partner with to develop and implement the plan?
- Are there clients or business partners who should be part of the planning process?
- Are there any outside stakeholders who can and should help develop the plan?
- Who needs to be involved to help get buy-in?

## Analyzing the Situation

The situation analysis is a summary of key issues relevant to the communication. It provides a brief, informal analysis of the strengths, weaknesses, opportunities and threats concerning the situation. You may want to use the SWOT analysis matrix and questions introduced in Chapter 3 to help complete this section.

In addition to the SWOT matrix, here are some other questions you should consider asking to get a complete picture of the situation:

- What are the basic facts of the situation?
- What do employees want?
- What matters most to the organization?
- Why is the organization in this situation?
- Why is the organization pursuing this course of action?

- How does the situation fit in with the organization's strategies?

- Which points will resonate positively with various stakeholders?

- What about the situation poses particular difficulties? Where are the potential conflicts? What points will be tough to sell to employees?

- Are their labor unions or other interest groups that have viewpoints on the situation? What are those viewpoints and how have they been expressed?

- Does this situation affect any external audiences? Does it impact customers, vendors or contractors?

- Are there areas where various stakeholders have conflicting needs or points of view?

- Is the situation confidential or highly sensitive?

- Are there any areas where more work or information is needed?

- What kind of research is needed in advance?


   The situation analysis is an opportunity for you, the project team and your internal clients to think through exactly what you're dealing with. It is also an opportunity to make sure everyone involved in the process agrees on exactly what the situation is. Sometimes it is surprising how different individuals have quite different perspectives on a situation that seems rather straightforward. If there isn't agreement between the employee communicators and their clients on exactly what the situation is, it is highly unlikely that the project will ever be seen as a success in the eyes of the client or organizational leaders.


## Determining the Objective

For purposes of this planning process, the objective is a simple overriding statement of what your organization is trying to achieve. The objective should be detailed enough to drive the plan's strategies. A well thought-out situation analysis should lead to a clear objective. You should ensure the entire project team and other key stakeholders agree on exactly what the objective is to prevent misunderstandings and problems, such as scope creep, later on. Just like the situation analysis, if there isn't agreement from the key stakeholders on the objective, it is unlikely your internal clients or organization's leaders will see the plan as successful no matter how it turns out.

Here are the types of questions you should consider when writing the objective:

- What are we truly trying to accomplish?
- What does success look like and why is it meaningful to the organization?
- What is the plan's purpose?
- What outcomes do we ultimately want to achieve?
- What does the situation analysis suggest about the objective?

✔ **PROCESS CHECK:** Once the objectives section is completed, it is a good idea for you and the project team to return to the title section and make any modifications necessary to align the objective and the title.

## Setting the Goals

The goals section outlines how you and the project team will know whether the objective was achieved. Put simply, the goals make the objective measurable. Goals put more detailed parameters around the objective. Goals must be measurable quantifiably, and they should be time-bound with a deadline. The goals must be directly related to the objective. They can be thought of as mile-markers on the journey toward the objective.

Here are some questions you should answer when formulating goals:

- How will we know we've succeeded? What specific things will happen?
- What do we want to put at stake to ensure we meet our objective?
- What can be measured? What metrics are available to us? What measures matter to the business?
- What goals will help ensure we meet the objective?
- What can we truly control? What measures are tied directly to this effort and are not impacted by other factors or noise?

✔ **PROCESS CHECK:** Once the strategies and tactics section (later in this document) are completed, you and the project team should return to this goals section and answer these questions: Are all your goals supported by the strategies? Are there strategies you devised that suggest additional goals you hadn't previously listed?

## Analyzing the Target Audience

Target audiences are the key stakeholders that need to interact with the communication. The target audience section should not be thought of as just a list of various employee audiences, but rather as an analysis. The target audience section is an opportunity for you to think through the size of various audiences, what matters to them, what's the appropriate method of communicating with them and what are their preferred methods of communication. A well thought-out audience analysis will help lead you and the project team to strategies and tactics, as well as the key messages you'll need to construct for each audience.

Target audiences should be defined narrowly. The employee communicators must make sure each important audience is covered. Forgotten audiences can be a major contributor to the failure of an otherwise great communication plan. Conversely, identifying a previously unrecognized key audience can be the difference between a good communication plan and a great communication plan.

You'll also want to identify atypical audiences and give some thought to their information needs. For example, employee benefit information is typically sent to employees, but frequently, their spouses are the decision-makers for the family's benefit selections. Identifying spouses as a target audience could lead to an innovative tactic. Perhaps employee spouses could be invited to attend an employee benefit fair where healthcare, 401(k) and other benefit vendors could be on hand to answer questions. The fair could be held after work hours so spouses could attend. A spouse who has a favorable opinion of an organization can influence overall employee satisfaction.

Many U.S.-based companies also have international employees so you should be mindful of their information needs. There may be language and cultural considerations and other important differences. For example, Canadian employees would not be eligible for a 401(k) plan because that is a provision under U.S. tax law; European employees might not understand non-metric measurements; and a reference to "summer" would be "winter" for employees south of the equator. Employee communicators who fail to be sensitive to international differences risk alienating these employees.

Contract employees are often excluded from internal communication, but they are often involved in key aspects of important projects. It often is a good idea to have them just as informed and supportive of the business objectives as regular employees.

In addition to the aforementioned audiences, the target audience section also is a good time to consider any external audiences such as the news media, investors, union officials, job seekers, retirees and the community. Although this book and this strategic plan approach is first and foremost concerned with employee audiences, it is the responsibility of the internal communication professional writing the communication plan to identify all target audiences, including specific external audiences, and to notify appropriate communication team members of the information needs of any of these external audiences.

Once you and the project team have determined all the target audiences, you should list each of them in priority order. The prioritization will help keep activities properly focused. The communicators and the project team may want to categorize the various audiences as primary, secondary or tertiary.

Here are some questions you should address when determining target audiences:

- Who is the proposed communication targeted to and why is each audience identified important?
- What do we want the audience to do, think, feel or believe as a result of this communication?
- What matters to the audience's members? What are they interested in? What do they value? What is likely to motivate them? What are they skeptical about?
- How does the audience's members want to be communicated with? What channels can you use to reach them? What are they likely to pay attention to? What will they ignore? What's credible to them?
- What level and frequency of communication do they need?
- What kinds of media do they consume outside of work?
- Are there sub-groups of any audience that have different needs and viewpoints?

- Will any audience members also be called upon to communicate the message? How will that impact the messages and the timing of the communication?

- What kinds of communication has the organization used to engage with the audience in the past? What does the audience think about the situation today?

- What's in it for each audience?

- Are there any audiences that should not be communicated with and why?

- Are there constraints of geography, time zones, work shifts, language, culture or technology with any of these audiences?

- Do we need more research?

## Crafting Key Messages

Key messages are the three to five message points that tell the story employees should remember. Key messages help ensure message clarity and consistency. They should be open and honest. Each key message must be credible to employees. Messages that have no credibility are worthless. In fact, one key message that isn't believable can undermine an entire communication effort. Key messages should support the communication plan objective and also be aligned with overarching internal brand messaging.

Well-done key messages can become the fountainhead for all communication materials so it is important to craft them carefully. You should be able to take a set of completed key messages and use them to create a letter from the CEO, a newsletter article, talking points for frontline supervisors, bullet points for a PowerPoint slide, a script for a video, and so on. Obviously, the key messages will have to be modified slightly so they are appropriate for the specific communication channel and specific format.

When developing key messages, keep in mind that external sources, such as the news media, are de facto employee communications because employees watch TV news and read newspapers, magazines and blogs. Therefore, external messaging and internal strategies should be aligned. Here's an example of how an external message contained in a press release can be modified to align it with internal strategies:

- **Original External Message:** "Our highly successful year is the result of the improving economy and the implementation of our expansion strategy."
- **Modified External Message:** "Our highly successful year is the result of the improving economy, the implementation of our expansion strategy and a lot of hard work by our dedicated employees."

At the same time, employees are their organizations' informal ambassadors; therefore, internal messaging should be aligned with external strategies. Organizations want their employees to carry their messages to family, friends and others in the community. Lastly, you should remember that communications intended solely for employees can be leaked to the news media and other external sources by accident or intentionally. Therefore, every internal communication should be written as if it will be seen and possibly quoted by the news media or other external sources. An infamous example of what can happen when an embarrassing internal memo gets leaked to the external world is detailed in Chapter 6, but for now, here are some questions for you to consider when crafting key messages:

- What three to five points do we want each target audience to retain?
- What matters most to the target audiences? What is most likely to resonate? What will be memorable?
- What language can we use to make the message connect with the audience and be memorable?
- What proof points, reasons to believe, stories, illustrations or anecdotes will be valuable?
- What content and tone is appropriate for the brand, the situation, the audience and the tool or person delivering the message?
- Have we covered all the major points (who, what, when, where, why and sometimes how)?
- How can we be most clear and concise?
- Are there points only some audiences need to know?
- What will those who disagree with the message say about it?

✔ **PROCESS CHECK:** Once this section has been completed, you and the project team should match up the key messages against the previously identified target audiences. Are there audiences that need specific messaging? Were any key messages created that now suggest additional audiences? Because strategies and tactics may guide and change key messages, you should return to this section after completing the next section and recheck the key messages.

**Figure 5.3: Strategies vs. Tactics**

| Strategies | Tactics |
| --- | --- |
| Methods, broad approaches, ideas. | Specific actions. |
| Big picture ideas that can be used in many situations. | Small picture perspective that is specific to a particular situation. |
| Timeless ideas not bound by technology. | Ideas that are often bound by current technology. |
| Example: Personalize the situation. | Use employee testimonials on the website. |

# Devising Strategies and Tactics

Many definitions of strategies and tactics exist in various business writings. For this communication plan's purposes, strategies are the overarching methods or broad approaches used to achieve the plan's objective and goals, and tactics are the particular actions used to implement the strategies. Put even more simply, strategies are ideas that drive an outcome and tactics are specific actions taken. In warfare, a surprise attack is a strategy, but the way in which it is carried out has changed over the years due to available technology. We've gone from ambushing from behind trees to an assault with night vision goggles, but the element of surprise remains the same. Figure 5.3 shows a further comparison between strategies and tactics.

As shown in Figure 5.4, each goal of the strategic communication plan should be supported by one or more strategies and one or more tactics should support each strategy.

**Figure 5.4 Goals, Strategies and Tactics Relationships**

Let's suppose we have an objective of increasing employee engagement. Our goal might be to increase the organization's overall score by 10 percentage points on its annual survey that measures employee engagement. One of the strategies that supports that goal is to increase opportunities for employees to participate in peer-to-peer communications. That strategy might cause us to think of a number of tactics. One might be to deploy an internal social media platform such as Yammer; another might be to activate the feature on the SharePoint intranet site called My Sites that allows employees to post updates about their project-related activities.

Strategies are quite often an outgrowth of the situation analysis and target audience analysis. You and your project team should go back and review those sections before drafting the strategies and tactics. You likely will do most of your thinking about the plan in this section. The better the strategies, the better the chance of the plan producing results that are not only measurable, but meaningful to the organization.

Tactics are the specific things you need to do to implement the strategy. Typically, several tactics will support one strategy. A collection of several related tactics might unveil a broader strategy. Form should follow function. The form your tactic takes should follow the strategic function. The communication matrix discussed in Chapter 4 will be helpful for this section.

Tactics are actions, but they are not detailed action steps. Let's say the tactic is to deploy an internal social media channel. You then will have to develop a detailed action plan that includes specific steps, deadlines and who is responsible for implementing each step.

Action steps might include sourcing and procuring the software, deploying the software, developing an online program to teach employees how to use the software, developing an internal marketing program to promote the use of the channel, and so on. Developing the action plan and timeline is covered in the next section.

✔ **PROCESS CHECK:** Are there tactics supporting each strategy? If there is a tactic you and the project team know they want to do, brainstorm the reasons why it is a good tactic. This process may reveal the true strategy and lead to even better strategies and tactics.

Confusion between strategies and tactics is a commonly made communication plan mistake. Correctly identifying which is which can facilitate creative thinking and create more effective communication plans. The following questions and examples will help employee communicators and the project team to understand the differences and allow them to create better strategies and tactics:

- What's the best way to approach this problem? What's the one thing we can do that will make it most likely that we achieve the objective? (This may lead to several strategies.)
- How can we make the most of the strengths and opportunities? How can we mitigate the weaknesses and threats?
- What does the audience analysis tell us about what will work for each target audience?
- What communication channels do we have at our disposal and how can we best use them?
- What strategies have we seen effectively employed in the past? How do they apply here? How do they need to be shifted?
- What brand-new ideas can we use?
- Once we understand our strategies, what are the next logical actions (tactics) to take?
- What strategy do the tactics you have in mind imply?

**Figure 5.5: Communication Breakthrough**

**Store Operations Manager:** A screen saver doesn't seem very personal or very inspirational. The only computer is in the store director's office so most frontline employees won't see it.

**Director of Internal Communication:** A video or something auditory would be more personal and hearing directly from the CEO surely would be more inspirational. He could say how much he appreciates how hard they are working and let them know how important it is to keep customer service levels up even though they are busy. But how can we get the message seen or heard by frontline employees?

**Store Operations Manager:** Most of the store computers don't have sound cards. But we could send a blast voicemail to all store directors. At least that way we'd have sound and a real human voice. And hey, maybe the store director could hold the intercom microphone up to the speakerphone and play the CEO message over the loudspeaker system throughout the store. Some store directors might forget to do it and the quality wouldn't be great, but at least we could get the message to most employees.

**Director of Internal Communication:** I'd never considered the store intercom as an employee communication channel. But wouldn't customers hear the message too?

**Store Operations Manager:** True, but we could play it in the morning before the store opens. All the employees are there an hour early stocking shelves and getting everything ready for the day. They usually have the Muzak system turned up really loud so they have something to listen to while they are working.

**Director of Internal Communication:** The Muzak system! What if we could record the message and have it played as part of the Muzak programming. Then it would be of a much higher quality and it would have much more of a surprise effect. Also, we'd be assured that the message was played at every store.

- If internal clients already have a tactic in mind, why do they like that particular tactic? What do they think it will achieve? (This might lead to a strategy and even better tactics.)
- Is this action something we do (tactic) or an idea that drives an outcome (strategy)?

Brainstorming strategies and tactics can sometimes lead to breakthrough thinking and communication magic. Figure 5.5 is an example of a brainstorm session involving the Director of Internal Communication and a Store Operations Manager at the fictional ABC Retail Co. It is based on a real life example. The two have been charged with devising an idea to deliver an uplifting message from the CEO to inspire frontline store employees during the busy holiday season. As is so often the case, no funding is being allocated for the project. It had been suggested that they deploy a screen saver to store computers containing some sort of holiday message, but they were free to devise another plan as long as it didn't cost anything other than their staff time.

The two did some checking with their Muzak representative and discovered that Muzak could indeed insert an audio message from the CEO as part of its programming. Muzak's system is even adjusted for time zones, assuring that the message would be played at 7 a.m. local time throughout the company. Other than staff time, the cost was nothing. The holiday message was delivered successfully via the Muzak system and spot checks with a dozen stores and unsolicited feedback from a dozen more showed store employees had a positive response to the message and its creative delivery.

The director of internal communication and the store operations manager decided to take this new employee communication channel one step further. Using radio commercials as an example, they created a series of 30 and 60-second spots containing employee messages. The following is an example of one such spot:

Did you know that ABC is one of just a few retailers in the nation that offers health benefits to its part-time employees? That's right. Even if you work less than 30 hours a week, you are still eligible for health benefits that can offer you care if you become sick or injured. You can find out all the details on your company intranet.

To add variety, they recorded each of 12 messages three times, once using a male voice, once using a female voice, and once using male and female voices alternating each sentence. They were able to locate two employees who were willing to lend their pleasant sounding voices for the spots; one had even been a former disc jockey. They were able to use a departmental digital recorder and free online sound editing software to create professional sounding spots. They essentially created a new employee communication channel that reached frontline employees with audio for no cost to their company.

It took both of them, working together, to come up with the breakthrough idea and to determine how to make it a reality.


## Drafting the Action Plan and Timeline

The action plan and timeline includes the nitty-gritty details to carry out each of the strategic communication plan tactics. This is the section that allows you and the project team to think through the details of implementing the plan and try to uncover what could go wrong. You need to think through everything that needs to happen, what contingencies to plan for, and where there are dependencies. Action plans should outline who is responsible for each step and when it needs to be completed. Figure 5.6 is a template that could be used to create an action plan and timeline.

Action plans are living documents. You should review and update the action plan and timeline daily during the implementation of a plan to uncover potential problems and thwart them before they occur. The project team should review the progress whenever it meets. The action steps and timeline can determine the success or failure in achieving the objective. After all, a plan is just words on paper unless someone takes action. The action plan and timeline also can help ensure flawless execution of the plan, and that will build credibility for you and the internal communication function.

Here are some questions to consider when drafting an action plan and timeline:

- What are the detailed steps needed to complete each tactic?

- Who is going to do the work? Do we have the necessary resources to implement the plan? Can we hire outside help if needed?

**Figure 5.6: Action Plan and Timeline Template**

| DUE DATE | ACTION ITEM | PERSON RESPONSIBLE | COMPLETED |
|---|---|---|---|
| TACTIC: | | | |
| | | | |
| | | | |
| | | | |
| TACTIC: | | | |
| | | | |
| | | | |
| TACTIC: | | | |
| | | | |
| | | | |
| | | | |

- How many working days (excluding weekends and holidays) do we have to complete the project?
- Are there timing issues? What steps must be completed before we can move on?
- Where are the potential roadblocks? What are the contingencies we need to plan for? What could go wrong?
- Are there any dependencies on other workgroups?
- Are there any interim steps we need to take?
- What are we missing?

## Formulating the Budget

The budget portion of the strategic communication plan provides a detailed summary of estimated and actual costs (if available) for all activities. You should go through each step of the action plan and timeline with the project team and identify which items will incur an expense. Each item that has costs associated with it should be included in the budget section of the template as shown in Figure 5.7. The budget section should reflect how your organization records projects. For example, the template could include cost center numbers and general ledger charge codes to help track costs during the project and refer back to in the future. In many organizations, internal clients pay for communication materials from their own budgets. You also may want to calculate Return On Investment (ROI) for the most expensive items on the action item list to help justify their need and to set appropriate expectations for how long it will take to see a positive effect.

Like the action plan and timeline, the budget also is a living document that will need to be updated as actual expenses are accrued. Once employee communicators have several completed projects documented with communication plans, they can begin to use the actual incurred costs to estimate costs on plans they are devising. Internal clients will often ask you to estimate a potential project's cost. How much does it cost to make a 10-minute video? How much will it cost to mail the brochure to employee homes? How much will it cost to print a four-page, four-color newsletter distributed to all employees? How much will it cost to develop a microsite on the intranet? The more you work with project budgets, the better you will become at estimating costs.

**Figure 5.7: Budget Template**

| ITEM | ESTIMATED COST | ACTUAL COST | COST CENTER CHARGED | G/L CODE |
|------|----------------|-------------|---------------------|----------|
|  |  |  |  |  |
|  |  |  |  |  |
|  |  |  |  |  |
|  |  |  |  |  |
|  |  |  |  |  |
|  |  |  |  |  |
|  |  |  |  |  |
|  |  |  |  |  |
|  |  |  |  |  |
|  |  |  |  |  |
|  |  |  |  |  |
|  |  |  |  |  |
| TOTAL: |  |  |  |  |
| ROI: |  |  |  |  |

Here are some questions to consider when formulating a proposed budget for a communication project:

- Which items on the action plan and timeline will incur an expense?
- To what budget will they be charged? Is the project part of a larger budget? How does it fit in?
- Do you need to hold aside budget dollars to handle the unexpected?
- How can you lower costs?
- Is there a Return on Investment (ROI) that can be calculated?
- Who needs to review and approve the budget for this project?
- What is the total estimated expense of the project?
- What are the costs associated with not communicating (such as legal fines, lost productivity, inefficient benefit plan utilization or increased employee turnover)?

## Evaluating the Plan

As an internal communicator, you typically are juggling multiple projects at the same time, so when one is completed, it is often tempting to skip the evaluation stage and get on with the next project or crisis de jour. But if you don't take the time to evaluate your plans, you'll never know how effective your plans were and you won't know whether any messages need to be recast or any other parts of your plan need to be refreshed. Evaluating how effective the plan was allows you to quantify the value of your internal communication efforts. Those values are typically significant, but often overlooked by the organization, largely because communicators fail to measure effectiveness or communicate their evaluation with the organization's leaders.

The evaluation plan should include the steps needed to measure whether the program has met its goals and objective. This section must be completed before beginning communication program implementation. That's because evaluation often requires pre-testing, informal surveying, benchmarking and other methods to establish a baseline of data for things such as employee attitudes and awareness. Employee communicators and the project team must take time to think through how they will measure the plan's success. They may need to plan for the evaluation in the budget and timeline sections.

Communication is by definition a two-way process, so all internal communication materials should include some method for employees to provide feedback or ask a question. This can be as simple as a "For more information, contact ..." line. The anecdotal feedback provided and the questions generated from a communication should become a part of the evaluation program as well.

If a goal is missed or only partially achieved, you should conduct a post-mortem analysis and include the findings in a written plan so future plans can be improved.

Here are some questions to consider when formulating an evaluation plan:

- What systems do we need to put in place now to ensure we can effectively measure the plan?

- Will these systems require staff resources or budget allocation?

- Are there other measurement systems in place already that we can use?

- Is evaluation included in our action plan?

- How can we ensure we achieve an accurate and objective evaluation of the project?

- Are there soft measures (such as teamwork in executing the plan) that we need to evaluate?

- What are we going to measure (e.g., message effectiveness, business impact)?

- Will we measure changes in awareness, depth of understanding, perceptions, attitudes, beliefs, workplace behaviors, commitment or level of employee engagement?

- Who will measure? Will we do it ourselves or engage a third-party expert?

- How will we measure – anecdotal feedback, focus groups, online polls, digital analytics, surveys, and communication audits?

✔ **PROCESS CHECK:** You should ensure that each item in the goals section is being measured in some way. Conversely, if you and the project team predetermined areas you plan to measure, you should ensure there is a corresponding goal. If there are things that are easily measurable but don't support goals, you should consider making them goals. For instance, if you know you are going to measure attendance at an employee event, you should consider setting a goal for how many attendees you and your internal client hope to attract. Also, at this stage of the plan, you and your project team should re-read the situation analysis to make sure you are addressing all the issues identified in the project evaluation.

> Communication is by definition a two-way process, so all internal communication materials should include some method for employees to provide feedback or ask a question.

## Determining the Project Approval Checklist

Making sure the appropriate people within your organization have reviewed and approved your strategic communication plan is important to the plan's success. A good review process, involving subject matter experts, will make the plan better. The people affected by the plan may have ideas you and the project team didn't identify. In addition, having the plan reviewed and approved may smooth out any workplace misunderstandings or office politics. If the right people support a plan early on, it will have a much better chance at succeeding.

The project approval checklist includes everyone in the organization who needs to review the proposed communication materials and in what order they need to approve them. Figure 5.7 shows a sample project approval checklist. The checklist should include all key stakeholders, collaborators and content experts. The project approval checklist can be used to think through how the plan will be executed, and also how you and the project team will gain support for and ownership of the plan. Those implementing the plan don't want to discover that a key stakeholder didn't get a chance to review materials beforehand because this situation can torpedo an otherwise sound plan in the midst of implementation.

**Figure 5.7: Action Plan and Timeline Template**

Project Team Leader and Director of Internal Communication
Name_____ Date_____

Vice President of Corporate Communications
Name_____ Date_____

Director of Payroll
Name_____ Date_____

Director of Compensation and Benefits
Name_____ Date_____

Senior Vice President of HR
Name_____ Date_____

Chief Financial Officer and Executive Sponsor
Name_____ Date_____


Some organizations have a system for projects where a Project Champion or Executive Sponsor is named. Those individuals may act as a liaison between the project team and the senior leadership team. These liaison positions can be helpful in obtaining broad support for the plan.

You may want to include signature lines within the plan document for each key plan reviewer to sign. The physical act of signing sometimes can help connote the importance of a thorough review by those individuals and imply that adherence to approval deadlines is important and expected.

Organizations frequently have some project approval processes already in place as part of how they do business. For instance, the senior leadership team may have a policy that it reviews all capital projects over a specified dollar amount or the IT team may have a governance committee that reviews all capital projects to determine the impact on IT systems. You need to be aware of these processes and know when proceedings are held (e.g., monthly or bi-monthly) so you can build them into your action plans and timelines. For example, if a governance committee only meets quarterly and you missed presenting your capital project by a week, you'll have to wait until the next one, which will delay your project by nearly three months.

> Internal communication professionals understand that their roles are not just to manage and lead the broad-based communications, but also to facilitate communication within the project team itself and upward to the organization's leadership.

In addition to getting approval and gaining support for a plan before it is launched, you should think about how often you should report plan progress to the plan's sponsors and the senior leadership team. It is important to maintain these lines of communication throughout a project's implementation to ensure its continued support. Internal communication professionals understand that their roles are not just to manage and lead the broad-based communications, but also to facilitate communication within the project team itself and upward to the organization's leadership. As an internal communication professional, you are in a perfect position to devise processes to keep everyone informed of the plan's progress. You may set up update processes, design progress report templates or suggest project team communication tools, such as a SharePoint team site.

In Chapter 10, we'll look at the evaluation of strategic communication plans and ways to measure communication plans' effectiveness in greater detail.

## Putting It All Together

Figure 5.8 is an example of a comprehensive internal communication strategic plan that was created for a public school system using the methodology detailed in this chapter. The plan is designed to assist the school district in enhancing its overall approach to internal communication in conjunction with a system-wide transformation initiative.

Figure 5.8: Sample Internal Communication Strategic Plan

## DEPARTMENT OF EDUCATION

# "Strive Higher"

## Internal Communication Strategic Plan 2014-2015
## February 22, 2013

### Project Team:
**Frank Johnson, Assistant Superintendent**
**Sally Wong, High School Principal**
**Thomas Goode, Classroom Teacher**
**Dirk Gonzales, Director of Information Systems**
**Elizabeth Greene, Manager of Internal Communication**

### SITUATION ANALYSIS

- The infrastructure for internal communication at DOE is fractured and weak. For instance, the organization does not have the ability to send a blast e-mail to all employees and there currently is no system-wide intranet.

- Staff resources are very limited and there is no one person dedicated to communicating to the organization's 25,000 employees. The organization's communicators are overwhelmed handling highly visible external communication and reacting to day-to-day crises. Even with the proper tools, it will be difficult for the current staff to implement them.

- Specific processes, procedures, protocols and guiding principles for handling internal communication have not been established.

- E-mail messages generally do not take full advantage of an HTML format with embedded links and graphics.

- The Superintendent's Info Exchange newsletter has been a valiant effort to consolidate internal messaging, but its newsletter format is designed to communicate tactical information and it does not allow for line-of-sight from teachers to key DOE priorities and high-level strategies. Instead, employees often receive information about major initiatives from external sources including the *Honolulu Star-Advertiser* and *Civil Beat*, both of which have reporters assigned to cover education.

- There are leadership meetings for Complex Area Superintendents that provide good information on priorities and initiatives, but there is no formal tool to assist these leaders to put the information into proper context and to cascade it to their direct reports and beyond.

- There are significant gaps in understanding, support and engagement of DOE's transformation efforts among principals, teachers and other employees. Employees do not see how various transformation initiatives tie together.

- Although some polling and surveying has been conducted, there are no ongoing feedback mechanisms in place for employees and no ongoing mechanisms to determine the effectiveness of internal communication.

## OBJECTIVE

- Create a robust internal communication system that engages employees to support fully and work actively for the organization's success and its transformation efforts.

## GOALS

Our goals are to have:

1. Clear, consistent, timely, accurate, relevant and candid internal communication delivered through effective communication channels.

2. Adequate resources available so internal communication needs can be met.

3. An internal communication function that operates smoothly and efficiently even in crisis situations.

4. Employees who have a deep understanding of organizational strategies, priorities and key initiatives.

5. Strong employee support for the organization's transformation efforts.

6. Widespread employee participation in the communication process.

7. Feedback mechanisms for employees and methods to measure the effectiveness of internal communication.

## TARGETED AUDIENCES

- Salaried personnel (22,500)
- Teachers (13,000)
- Education officers, including principals, assistant principals (900)
- Classified employees, including custodians and cafeteria workers (8,600)
- Complex Area Superintendents
- Board of Education
- Union Leadership
- Consultants working on DOE transformation projects

## KEY MESSAGES

- The world around us has changed and the demands on education have never been greater. The public expects us to be successful with all students. Public perception is that we are failing to meet that goal. We cannot continue operating our education system the same way.
- Even the very best of today will not be good enough for tomorrow. We must strive higher.
- We are transforming into a modern educational system to meet the needs of students today and in the future. This transformation is critical to our graduates' success and Hawaii's economic future.
- Our transformation efforts are consistent with the leading-edge thinking in education throughout the nation.
- We are striving to achieve results never before accomplished, so we will need to employ methods we have never before attempted. This may be uncomfortable at times, but it is also exciting.

- As with any major change, there will be ups and down along the way. And, as with anything that is new, there will be risks. But the biggest risk of all is doing nothing. We cannot afford to keep doing the same thing. Our students deserve our very best.
- We have good strategies and a sound plan in place to take us where we need to be. We can do this but it will take everyone—the administration, principals, teachers, support staff, students, parents and the community—working together to succeed.
- Change is never easy and it will take time to accomplish all we need to do. The length of time it takes to move our education system forward can be frustrating at times. The key to success is our ability to rally together and stay the course until the work is done.

## STRATEGIES AND TACTICS

**Goal #1:** Have clear, consistent, timely, accurate, relevant and candid internal communication delivered through effective communication channels.

- **Strategy:** Optimize and enhance existing tools.
  **Tactics:**
  - Create a DOE e-mail box with the display name "DOE Communications" as a unified message platform for all official system-wide communication to employees.
  - Source and deploy an e-mail management system that will allow the sending of blast e-mails as well as audience-specific e-mails. It also will enable click-through tracking to get a true measure of readership.
  - Provide key messaging on a regular basis for schools to repurpose in their own newsletters and other communication.
  - Ensure internal messages are coordinated with external messages.

- **Strategy:** Create a cohesive look and feel for all broad-based internal communication.
  **Tactics:**
  - Apply the Strive Higher brand look to all internal communication. Create templates for PowerPoint, newsletters and HTML e-mails.
  - Redesign the Superintendent's Info Exchange newsletter, the DOE News Service e-mail and all other appropriate communication in the Strive Higher look.

- **Strategy:** Leverage web-based technologies (when SharePoint site is deployed).
  **Tactics:**
  - Hire SharePoint consultants to create internal marketing plan for SharePoint portal designed to generate excitement from employees and educate them about basic SharePoint features.
  - Push DOE and industry news content to MySites on a daily basis or use blast e-mail.
  - Produce weekly podcast interviews with content experts. Archive them by topic and cross-reference in other communication channels as appropriate.
  - Produce monthly webcast from the superintendent to discuss major initiatives. Listeners would be encouraged to ask questions.
  - Post video clips and photos of all major events. Create an online archive.
  - Encourage readers to submit video clips and photos. Consider a "Photo of the Day" and / or "Video of the Week."
  - Allow users to "Like" content as a feedback mechanism.

**Goal #2:** Have adequate resources available so internal communication needs can be met.
- **Strategy:** Shift staffing priorities and increase existing staff so internal communication needs can be met.
  **Tactics:**
  - Reassess job descriptions, optimize processes, eliminate any unnecessary duties, and determine what outside resources are available.
  - Create a new internal communication specialist position focused primarily on internal communication. This position will be crucial in implementing this plan. The ideal candidate for this position would have a degree in journalism, public relations, organizational communication or a related field; 3-5 years of experience in internal communication; strong writing and editing skills; highly developed computer skills; experience in managing a SharePoint intranet portal; experience in event planning; and experience in education communication.

- Shift the duties of the webmaster or other appropriate IT position to function as a SharePoint administrator. This position will work with and support the communication team with technical solutions to the SharePoint portal.

**Goal #3:** Have an internal communication function that operates smoothly and efficiently even in crisis situations.
- **Strategy:** Determine roles and responsibilities, and design procedures, processes, protocols and guiding principles for handling internal communication.

  **Tactics:**
  - Review job descriptions, document procedures, flow-chart processes, and write protocols and guiding principles.
  - Ensure external communication is in sync with internal messaging.

**Goal #4:** Have employees who have a deep understanding of organizational strategies, priorities and key initiatives.
- **Strategy:** Use DOE senior leadership to connect the organization's vision with employees.

  **Tactics:**
  - Ensure the leadership meeting is held annually before the start of the new school year. Agenda will celebrate successes from the previous year, set the tone for the coming year and highlight key strategies. This will help create a direct line-of-sight to DOE's vision and key initiatives, achieve buy-in and energize attendees. It also allows for training opportunities and networking.
  - Create a "Breakfast with the Superintendent" where the superintendent could share information on current initiatives and solicit feedback from a cross section of employees (principals, teachers and support staff). A report summarizing the discussion would be posted to the SharePoint intranet.
  - Schedule leader walk-arounds at schools to share information on current initiatives and to solicit feedback.

- **Strategy:** Provide Complex Area Superintendents (CASs) and Principals with communication tools.

    **Tactic:**

    - Create a written talking points document that CASs can use as a monthly discussion guide when they hold face-to-face meetings with their principals. The written guide will help ensure consistency of key messages, make the messages relevant, allow for feedback and provide a structure to the meetings. Principals would be encouraged to cascade the messages to their teachers and record feedback that can be reported back up to the CAS.

**Goal #5:** Have strong employee support for the organization's transformation efforts.

- **Strategy:** Make the case for change, show how the pieces fit together, demonstrate how employees can contribute to the success of the transformation effort and build a better future for students.

    **Tactics:**

    - Share Internal Communication Plan and Strive Higher plan with DOE leadership and transformation consultants to ensure unified approaches and messaging.
    - Launch the Strive Higher transformation initiative as the definitive long-term plan for education at the July 19 leadership meeting.
    - Brand all transformation initiatives under the Strive Higher banner.
    - Create supporting tools including FAQs, PowerPoint, suggested newsletter articles for schools and PDF posters.
    - Create transformation DVD that can be shared by principals with their teachers.
    - Model brand behavior by recognizing "Strive Higher Heroes" who are helping to lead the way.
    - Incorporate messaging into recruitment and new hire information. Assess all HR communication to look for further opportunities.
    - Create a Strive Higher Teamsite on the SharePoint intranet to centralize information and update progress.

**Goal #6:** Have widespread employee participation in the communication process.

– **Strategy:** Position the new SharePoint intranet as a virtual community that brings DOE together and fosters a vested interest in its success.

**Tactics:**

- Engage content experts to create and maintain a Glossary of Terms and Acronyms wiki.
- Engage content experts by interviewing them for weekly podcasts.
- Encourage all employees to create and personalize SharePoint MySites.
- Encourage employees working on team projects to collaborate by using SharePoint TeamSites.
- Encourage other departments to use content management, document retention, forms and transactional features of SharePoint.
- Continue to look for free webparts that can enhance SharePoint for things such as event sign-ups, calendars of events, employee directories, etc.
- Further engage employees through internal social media tools such as Yammer.
- Determine whether it makes sense to pursue an external social media strategy as a way to reach internal audiences.
- Employ "gamification" techniques to increase usage of the intranet. This could include the awarding of electronic badges and other techniques to reward readership.

**Goal #7:** Have feedback mechanisms for employees and methods to measure the effectiveness of internal communication.

– **Strategy:** Solicit feedback in all communication channels.

**Tactics:**

- All communication vehicles should include a statement of whom to contact for user submissions, comments or questions.
- All live presentations should include a Q&A.

– **Strategy:** Evaluate and measure communication effectiveness.

**Tactics:**

- Utilize measurement tools on all electronic tools on an ongoing basis to determine trends.
- Utilize polling capability of SharePoint when appropriate to gauge sentiment.

- When existing tools are revamped, conduct communication survey to gauge success. Conduct a follow-up survey about three months after new tools are launched to measure progress.
- Use a third-party communication measurement firm to conduct a comprehensive communication audit. The audit would include written surveys and focus groups for both qualitative and quantitative data. The data would be analyzed to determine the next steps in the development of the internal communication function.

## ACTION PLAN AND TIMEFRAMES

**Phase I** (Between now and the July 19, 2012, Leadership Meeting)
- Upon Adoption of Plan: All communication vehicles should include a statement of whom to contact for user submissions, comments or questions.
- Upon Adoption of Plan: All live presentations should include a Q&A.
- By May 31: Finalize the Internal Communication Strategic Plan.
- By June 8: Share Internal Communication Plan and Strive Higher plan with DOE leadership and transformation consultants.
- By June 22: Create Strive Higher supporting tools including FAQs, PowerPoint, suggested newsletter articles for schools and PDF posters.
- By June 29: Create templates for PowerPoint, newsletters and HTML e-mails.
- By June 29: Create Strive Higher transformation DVD that can be shared by principals with their teachers.
- By June 29: Advertise for Internal Communication Specialist position.

**Phase II:** (Between the July 19, 2012, Leadership Meeting and December 2012)
- July 19: Launch the Strive Higher transformation initiative and brand all transformation initiatives under the Strive Higher banner.
- Ready to go by July 20: Schedule leader walk-arounds at schools to share information on current initiatives and to solicit feedback.
- By July 31: Reassess job descriptions, optimize processes, eliminate any unnecessary duties, and determine outside resources.
- By July 31: Write job descriptions, document procedures, flow-chart processes, and write protocols and guiding principles.

- By August 3: Hire and onboard new Internal Communication Specialist.
- By August 31: Apply the Strive Higher brand look to all new internal communication. Redesign the Superintendent's Info Exchange newsletter, the DOE News Service e-mail and other appropriate system-wide communication.
- By September 28: Create a written talking points document that CASs can use as a monthly discussion guide.
- October: Work with HR to incorporate Strive Higher and other internal messaging into recruitment and new hire information.
- November: SharePoint consultants to begin drafting SharePoint portal internal marketing plan.
- December: Assess effectiveness of Strive Higher materials, CAS monthly discussion guide, redesigned newsletters and leader walk-arounds through informal focus groups, online survey (such as Survey Monkey) and performing an analysis of anecdotal feedback.
- December: Create a "Breakfast with the Superintendent" plan and schedule.

**Phase III** (January 2013 to July 2013)
- January: Launch monthly "Breakfast with the Superintendent."
- January: Launch internal marketing plan for SharePoint intranet portal.
- February: Deploy an e-mail management system and SharePoint portal. Begin utilizing measurement tools on all electronic tools on an ongoing basis to determine trends.
- March: Create a Strive Higher TeamSite on the SharePoint intranet to centralize information and update progress.
- April: Begin posting video clips and photo archives of all major events.
- April: Begin planning next leadership meeting.
- May: Assess effectiveness of "Breakfast with the Superintendent," SharePoint portal (including the Strive Higher TeamSite), and e-mail management tool.
- June: Finalize leadership meeting preparations.
- July: Leadership meeting.
- July: Model brand behavior by recognizing Strive Higher heroes who are helping to lead the way. (Could launch at the leadership meeting.)

**Phase IV** (Between August 2013 and December 2013)
- August: Launch two-month SharePoint MySite pilot program with CASs.
- September: Allow "Likes" as a feedback mechanism on SharePoint content.
- October: Upon successful pilot of MySites, encourage all employees to create and personalize SharePoint MySites.
- November: Begin pushing news content to SharePoint MySites in real time.
- December: Begin two-month SharePoint TeamSite pilot.

**Phase V** (January 2014 and July 2014)
- January: Begin producing weekly podcast interviews with content experts on what's new in areas such as food service, facilities, training, transportation and technology. Archive them by topic and cross reference in other communication channels as appropriate.
- February: Upon successful completion of TeamSite pilot, encourage employees working on team projects to collaborate by using SharePoint TeamSites.
- March: Engage content experts to create and maintain a Glossary of Terms and Acronyms wiki.
- April: Begin planning next leadership meeting.
- May: Assess effectiveness of MySites, TeamSites, podcasts and glossary wiki.
- June: Finalize leadership meeting preparations.
- July: Leadership meeting.

**Phase VI** (August 2014 to December 2014)
- August: Devise plan and schedule for monthly employee webcast from the superintendent to discuss major initiatives.
- September: Begin monthly webcasts from the superintendent.
- September: SharePoint administrator should look for additional free webparts that will enhance the SharePoint experience.
- October: SharePoint administrator should look for opportunities and encourage other departments to use content management, document retention, forms and transactional features of SharePoint.
- November: Assess effectiveness of monthly webcasts.
- December: Begin planning for comprehensive internal communication audit that would incorporate feedback from focus groups and written surveys.

## Phase VII (January 2015 to July 2015)

- January: Pilot employee polling capabilities through SharePoint portal.
- March: Launch employee polling through SharePoint portal.
- April: Begin planning next leadership meeting.
- May: Conduct comprehensive internal communication audit. (May want to report results at July leadership meeting.)
- June: Finalize leadership meeting preparations.
- July: Leadership meeting.

## Phase VIII (August 2015 and beyond)

- August: Revise Internal Communication Strategic Plan with data from audit.
- Incorporate dashboard plan into SharePoint portal.
- Consider employing "gamification" techniques to increase usage of the intranet.
- Consider engaging employees with internal social media tools such as Yammer.
- Determine whether it makes sense to pursue an external social media strategy as a way to reach internal audiences.

**KEY BUDGET ITEMS**

| ITEM | ESTIMATED COSTS | ACTUAL COST |
|---|---|---|
| Internal Communication Specialist | $50,000 annually | |
| Leadership meeting | $25,000 per meeting | |
| SharePoint intranet training and launch | $40,000 | |
| Podcast cost, including audio editing software and digital recorder | $400 | |
| E-mail management tool | $10,000 | |
| Communication Audit (2015) to be performed by a professional communication measurement firm—would include written surveys and focus groups for both qualitative and quantitative data | $20,000 | |

## EVALUATION PLAN

- Regular usage reports will be gathered from Google Analytics on the SharePoint site. This will include numbers of page visits, video and podcast downloads, and "Likes" and can be used to determine applicable content and location. A polling webpart also can be used to determine employee sentiments on specific topics.

- Ongoing measurement of e-mail click-throughs and anecdotal feedback will help determine whether readership is increasing.

- An evaluation on staffing requirements and the effectiveness of the internal communication function should be conducted annually by the leadership.

- Feedback collected through the Leadership Discussion Guide process and anecdotal feedback from the CASs will help determine whether messages are being received as intended and whether the process is working.

- The number of SharePoint MySites and TeamSites created, and the participation level in wikis and podcasts, will show the strategy's effectiveness to involve employees in the communication process.

- New communication channels should be assessed for effectiveness 2-3 months following rollout using informal focus groups, an online survey tool (such as Survey Monkey) and an analysis of anecdotal feedback.

- A comprehensive communication audit should be conducted in 2015 to ascertain the effectiveness of internal communication tools and determine the next steps.

# Chapter Conclusion

Strategic communication planning is part art and part science. The rigor of the process helps ensure flawless and efficient execution of the plan, and the methodology of creating the plan can facilitate creative thinking and may spawn breakthrough ideas. But ultimately, it is the individuals crafting the plan and implementing the action steps that will determine success. When the blend of the process, creativity and people is just right, breakthrough thinking and communication magic happens. As internal communication professionals, we live for those moments. They are exhilarating experiences that cause us to jump out of our chairs and do a happy dance. They don't happen every day and most certainly they don't happen without a strategic plan.

## Chapter Exercises

1. Explain the differences between strategies and tactics.

_____

_____

_____

2. Explain why it is important to know the difference between a strategy and a tactic.

_____

_____

_____

3. The weakest part of most strategic planning efforts is a failure to do what?

_____

_____

_____

# Chapter 6

# Finding the Voice of the Brand

"Humor can get in under the door while seriousness
is still fumbling at the handle."
– G.K. Chesterton

**Chapter Overview:** The tone of your communication is crucial to your message getting through and being interpreted by your employee audience in the way it is intended. One of your roles as an internal communication professional is to help your organization identify appropriate tones and develop a Voice of the Brand.

In this chapter, you'll learn various tones an organization could choose to use and you'll see how each choice could affect the effectiveness of your internal communication efforts. This information will give you ideas about how to choose the most appropriate tone for your communications and help you to develop an overall Voice of the Brand for your organization. Getting the Voice of the Brand just right will have a dramatic impact on the effectiveness of your communication efforts.

Just like people, organizations have personalities. An organization's personality is formed by a myriad of things that could include the type of industry it is in, the management style of its leaders, its specific business model, the type of employees it attracts, significant events in its history, its brand reputation, its formal policies and its unwritten rules. Perhaps an organization's industry is old and is steeped in tradition as are the banking, mining and railroad industries. Or perhaps it is in a high-tech industry like software development or aerospace. It could be an aggressive upstart organization, busy acquiring new companies and subsidiaries, or it could be a non-profit association or a branch of government. Maybe it is attracting Millennials or maybe it is heavily unionized. Perhaps the organization has been through a bankruptcy, a major merger or a major restructuring. It could be an organization trying to adapt for survival's sake or one going through a period of prosperity and rapid expansion. All of these things, and many more, can affect an organization's personality.

> The organizational voice used to deliver internal communication often is a direct reflection of the relationship an organization's leadership has with its employees.

One role of internal communication professionals is to understand the organization's personality and help establish the organization's voice. If that voice is to be effective, it must be credible. And to be credible, that voice must reflect the organization's personality. The organizational voice used to deliver internal communication often is a direct reflection of the relationship an organization's leadership has with its employees. Of course, like people, an organization adapts the tone of its voice to suit specific situations and specific communications. The tone could be adapted from lighthearted to serious as appropriate, but the organization's overall voice should be consistent.

An organization could use many tones to communicate with its employees. Figure 6.1 lists some common tones and their characteristics. Many factors could affect the tone used, including the specific audience being targeted, the situation, the intended action employees should take as a result of receiving the message, and the medium chosen to carry the message.

Let's look at each tone in more detail and discuss the ramifications of each as it relates to employee engagement and effective internal communication.

The parental tone typically accompanies a top-down communication from an organization's management to its employees, such as a memo from the

## Figure 6.1: Characteristics of Organizational Tones

| TONE | CHARACTERISTICS | COMMONLY USED WITH |
|---|---|---|
| Parental | Top-down communication with little or no opportunity for meaningful feedback. The tone seems to suggest that "management knows best," although it is often unintentional. | Management e-mails, memos, letters and in speeches, videos and podcasts. |
| Directive | Task-oriented and often dictatorial. Focused on the "what" not the "why." Aimed at achieving compliance and consistency. Limited or no opportunity for feedback. | Management e-mails, memos, letters and instructional videos. |
| Businesslike | Professional but impersonal. Often includes jargon and stilted business-speak. | Management e-mails, memos, letters and other written materials. |
| Legal | Legal but impersonal. Attempts to mitigate misinterpretations and misrepresentations but may be difficult to understand. | Management e-mails, memos and letters regarding matters of potential litigation. |
| Promotional | Sells ideas, internal events or internal offerings. Frequently oversells and thus loses credibility. | Posters, brochures and videos. |
| Informational | Standardized, sanitized, objective, accurate and factual, but often bland and uninteresting. | Organizational newsletters, intranet postings and other written communication. |
| Partner | Treats the audience as partners. Focuses on the "what" and the "why." Also encourages frequent feedback and peer-to-peer communication. | E-mails, e-letters, intranets and other digital communication, and podcasts, speeches and other spoken communication. |
| The Voice of the Brand | Reflects the organization's brand, including the organization's current and desired future states. | All communication channels. |

CEO. Note that I use the term "management" here as opposed to "leaders" because those who think of their role as managing their employees' actions rather than leading them are more apt to use a parental tone. The parental tone connotes that "management knows best." Usually little or no opportunity exists for meaningful feedback and the message insinuates "Just do it and don't ask questions."

Typically, the parental tone is intended to be directive or simply informative and the patronizing aspect of it is usually unintentional. Management may be intending to tell employees only what it believes they need to know to get their jobs done efficiently. A communicator who is sensitive to tone usually can turn a parental tone into a directive tone with a few simple edits.

> A parental tone may generate short-term results, but it will not build trust between employees and management, and it will not engage employees in the organization's long-term success.

Sometimes the parental tone is the inadvertent result of a feeling of mistrust on the part of the organization's management toward their employees. Management may be wary of giving employees too much information for fear of how they might interpret it.

A parental tone may generate short-term results, but it will not build trust between employees and management, and it will not engage employees in the organization's long-term success. In fact, if the tone belittles employees, it will have a decidedly negative impact on employee engagement.

Figure 6.2 shows a flier intended as a creative way to show employees working at the company's corporate headquarters the importance of securing their laptop computers after hours. Members of the IT Asset Management Team distributed the fliers after hours at the workstations of employees who had not secured their laptop computers. The IT folks even entered locked office doors in some cases. The following morning, there was an immediate backlash by employees who objected to the parental tone and the sneaky behavior. The message did get the attention of employees and it did make some points that needed to be made. However, it unnecessarily created an "us against them" feeling among employees.

The IT Asset Management Team had not consulted the internal communication professionals about its need to communicate information about securing laptops or its plan to distribute the flier, but its team members did call upon them following the uproar. They needed immediate damage control. The employee communicators devised a communication plan. Step 1 was to apologize for the poor communication. Next was a series of communications explaining the importance of securing laptops and offering IT training and support to install anti-theft cables. The tone changed from "You did something wrong" to "Let's work together to solve this important problem."

**Figure 6.2: Example of Unintentional Parental Tone**

Your laptop could have been

# "STOLEN"

by a member of the IT Asset Management Team because it was found to be left unsecured on your desk last night.

Your name will be part of the list given to your senior vice president showing which employees would have left XYZ Corporation's laptop/PDA assets unsecured within offices or cubicles.

As an employee who has been assigned this expensive, portable piece of equipment, it is your responsibility to ensure it is secure at all times, both when it is with you as well as when it is left in the office. As a reminder, laptops are never to be left in vehicles nor checked as baggage when traveling. If you choose not to lock it up in an overhead bin/drawer or take it home at night, we can give you a security cable to secure it to your desk. To request a security cable, fill out a request form on the intranet and we will give you a cable. Simply locking your office is not sufficient for keeping the laptop secure.

If you do not travel at least 35% of the time for your job, please submit a request form and the IT desktop team can get you set up with a desktop PC that is much more powerful. Loaner laptops are available for once in awhile trips and project needs. Your cooperation in the asset protection effort is required and greatly appreciated. The complete employee asset responsibility policy is on the back of this page.

There are times, however, when the parental tone is intentional, and in such cases, the organization probably has much bigger problems than just communication style. Figure 6.3 shows the infamous "tick-tock" e-mail sent in 2001 by Neal Patterson, CEO of Cerner Corp., to his 400 managers. Patterson lambasted his managers for not working hard enough. Within days of its issuance, the e-mail was leaked by someone and posted to several internet sites including a Yahoo! investor board. Soon the business world and internal communication professionals everywhere became aware of the CEO's ill-conceived rant. Patterson later apologized to his employees in a follow-up e-mail. As of this writing, Patterson was still the CEO of the medical software company.

Patterson probably didn't consult with his internal communication team before sending his notorious e-mail. If he had, they surely would have advised a different course of action starting with the fact that such a message should not be delivered via e-mail and reminding him of the internal communication guiding principle that says don't put anything out internally that you don't want to read in the news the next day.

It is doubtful the employee communicators could have talked Patterson out of the message entirely, but perhaps they could have helped him make his point about working harder in a more palatable manner. They may have been able to mitigate the damage by turning his parental tone into a directive tone and changed the delivery channel to a more appropriate one. A tough message like the one Patterson was trying to deliver usually goes over better in front of a live audience because those speaking can often sense how the message is being received and modify their tone on the spot. Also, the audience likely will feel more respected because "at least he had the guts to say it to our face." But sometimes, no matter what we do, we can't save CEOs from themselves.

## The Directive Tone

The directive tone is task-oriented and often dictatorial. Directive communications are professional, businesslike, direct and clear. Messages sometimes read like step-by-step instructions. The connotation of the directive tone is that management is telling employees exactly what they need to know—and nothing more. Management's focus is on what to do and not why employees are being asked to do it. Directive messages may

## Figure 6.3: Intentional Parental Tone

From: Patterson,Neal
To: DL_ALL_MANAGERS;
Subject: MANAGEMENT DIRECTIVE: Week #10_01: Fix it or changes will be made
Importance: High

To the KC_based managers:

I have gone over the top. I have been making this point for over one year.

We are getting less than 40 hours of work from a large number of our KC-based EMPLOYEES. The parking lot is sparsely used at 8AM; likewise at 5PM. As managers -- you either do not know what your EMPLOYEES are doing; or YOU do not CARE. You have created expectations on the work effort which allowed this to happen inside Cerner, creating a very unhealthy environment. In either case, you have a problem and you will fix it or I will replace you.

NEVER in my career have I allowed a team which worked for me to think they had a 40 hour job. I have allowed YOU to create a culture which is permitting this. NO LONGER.

At the end of next week, I am plan to implement the following:
1. Closing of Associate Center to EMPLOYEES from 7:30AM to 6:30PM.
2. Implementing a hiring freeze for all KC based positions. It will require Cabinet approval to hire someone into a KC based team. I chair our Cabinet.
3. Implementing a time clock system, requiring EMPLOYEES to 'punch in' and 'punch out' to work. Any unapproved absences will be charged to the EMPLOYEES vacation.
4. We passed a Stock Purchase Program, allowing for the EMPLOYEE to purchase Cerner stock at a 15% discount, at Friday's BOD meeting. Hell will freeze over before this CEO implements ANOTHER EMPLOYEE benefit in this Culture.
5. Implement a 5% reduction of staff in KC.
6. I am tabling the promotions until I am convinced that the ones being promoted are the solution, not the problem. If you are the problem, pack you bags.

I think this parental type action SUCKS. However, what you are doing, as managers, with this company makes me SICK. It makes sick to have to write this directive.

I know I am painting with a broad brush and the majority of the KC based associates are hard working, committed to Cerner success and committed to transforming health care. I know the parking lot is not a great measurement for 'effort'. I know that 'results' is what counts, not 'effort'. But I am through with the debate.

We have a big vision. It will require a big effort. Too many in KC are not making the effort.

I want to hear from you. If you think I am wrong with any of this, please state your case. If you have some ideas on how to fix this problem, let me hear those. I am very curious how you think we got here. If you know team members who are the problem, let me know. Please include (copy) Kynda in all of your replies.

I STRONGLY suggest that you call some 7AM, 6PM and Saturday AM team meetings with the EMPLOYEES who work directly for you. Discuss this serious issue with your team. I suggest that you call your first meeting -- tonight. Something is going to change.

I am giving you two weeks to fix this. My measurement will be the parking lot: it should be substantially full at 7:30 AM and 6:30 PM. The pizza man should show up at 7:30 PM to feed the starving teams working late. The lot should be half full on Saturday mornings. We have a lot of work to do. If you do not have enough to keep your teams busy, let me know immediately.

Folks this is a management problem, not an EMPLOYEE problem. Congratulations, you are management. You have the responsibility for our EMPLOYEES. I will hold you accountable. You have allowed this to get to this state. You have two weeks. Tick, tock

Neal Patterson
Chairman & Chief Executive Officer
Cerner Corporation www.cerner.com
2800 Rockcreek Parkway; Kansas City, Missouri 64117
"We Make Health Care Smarter"

often sound like they come from a benevolent dictator who seems to be saying: "You're too busy to want all the details anyway. Details would only serve to confuse you. So, here are just the facts you need to know."

The directive tone assumes that employees are not interested in strategies or that they will get that information from some other source.

> A tough message usually goes over better in front of a live audience because those speaking can often sense how the message is being received and modify their tone on the spot.

Above all else, the directive tone seeks compliance and consistent execution of tasks. Success is measured by compliance and flawless execution. Often, multiple directives are sent out and each says it is important and needs to be done as soon as possible. Often the receivers of such messages aren't given any context or a way to prioritize the work they are being asked to do. If an employee receives three directives at the same time, that employee will not know which to do first without some way to filter and prioritize the messages.

Directive communications seek limited or no feedback. If feedback is sought, it is usually restricted to information aimed at improving efficiency. Feedback about how employees feel is usually not sought or welcomed.

Like the parental tone, directive communications may generate short-term measurable results, but it likely will not engage employees, build trust or engender any long-term commitment to the organization.

## The Businesslike Tone

The businesslike tone is professional but impersonal. It seeks to convey importance and respect, and its purpose is to drive business results. The businesslike tone's effectiveness can become hampered by its inherent use of stilted business-speak, such as "per your request" or "leveraging our opportunities." The overuse of such terms can create a feeling of alienation between an organization's leadership and its employees. Employees may feel that "management just doesn't get it."

Using a businesslike tone also can put the credibility of communications at risk if the terminology is seen as purposely obfuscating a message's true meaning. For example, an organization that refers to a layoff as "a realignment" runs the risk of losing credibility unless the organization can make a valid case of why "realignment" is a better word choice than "layoff."

The businesslike tone is steeped in tradition, so when used, leaders may find themselves falling back on cliché business-speak when seeking ways to express themselves. It is up to savvy employee communicators who are sensitive to employee engagement and message credibility to suggest edits that can make the businesslike tone more palatable to employees.

Feedback is typically more open than in parental and directive toned communications, but businesslike communications usually regard feedback as being between the organization's leadership and its employees, and typically, it doesn't acknowledge or encourage peer-to-peer communication. Because of the risks of alienation and credibility, and because of the lack of peer-to-peer communication, the businesslike tone is not the best choice to engage employees and to achieve the most effective communication possible.

## The Legal Tone

The legal tone seeks to lower the legal exposure of a particular communication, but in doing so, it is impersonal, often difficult to understand and sometimes alienating to employees. Its aim is to reduce potential misinterpretations and misrepresentations. The legal tone is often combined with the businesslike tone and is commonly used for management memos and letters regarding matters of potential litigation or ongoing negotiations with collective bargaining units.

Sometimes, a communication's purpose is simply to fulfill a legal requirement and not to enlighten or engage employees. Nevertheless, an employee communicator who is skilled in writing and editing can usually find appropriate terminology to meet the legal needs of a communication and, at the same time, add enough warmth to prevent employee alienation.

But even with the best editing, the legal tone is not the best choice to engage employees or to produce the most effective communications possible.

## The Promotional Tone

The promotional tone tries to sell ideas, internal events or internal offerings. This tone is commonly used with internal marketing materials, such as posters and brochures, and is usually parroting external advertising and marketing campaigns. Amateur communicators often adopt a promotional tone to try to energize mundane ideas in order to sell them. They attempt to add more excitement to copy by using colorful adjectives and by overusing exclamation marks. A statement such as "Benefits Open Enrollment starts tomorrow!!!!" lacks credibility because employees won't find that fact to be exciting no matter how many exclamation marks are used. There are, however, important points about Benefits Open Enrollment that employees do need to know, such as that employees have the opportunity to pick the plans that best suit their and their families and loved ones' unique needs.

Another technique amateur communicators try to borrow from marketing campaigns are teasers to "build excitement." But this technique is only effective if the information revealed at the end of the teaser is truly exciting. Telling employees for weeks that "something big is coming" and then letting them down by finally revealing that the big something is a new intranet site for the safety department is not effective.

At its best, the promotional tone can result in compelling writing and could produce effective short-term results. But it typically attempts to tell the target audience what to think rather than asking for its feedback, or engaging it and allowing people to reach their own conclusions. The axiom "show, don't tell" should be applied to promotional writing. Employees know when they're being sold something and an overuse of the promotional tone can alienate employees. Furthermore, overselling and overpromising over and over makes it difficult for employees to prioritize what really is important and it dilutes messages about things that really are exciting.

# The Informational Tone

The informational tone is the primary tone for news reporting in the external world and many internal communicators adopt the same third-party objective perspective in an effort to impart facts in a professional manner. This use is particularly true when the communicators are writing a printed organizational newsletter because the frame of reference of such a channel is a newspaper. The informational tone is standardized by a strict adherence to a style guide, and it is sanitized by a reluctance to use adjectives for fear of losing objectivity and accuracy. Above all else, the fear is "We won't sound professional if we do that."

The problem is, the objective perspective, devoid of adjectives and colorful language, can be bland and uninteresting. It is common for internal clients to submit newsletter copy in a promotional tone and for them to be disappointed when the internal communication professionals edit the copy into an informational tone. The internal clients see the informational tone's professionalism, but they believe all the life has been sucked out of their message and they fear the communication's effectiveness will suffer as a result. They are right about one thing: if the copy isn't compelling, it will be less effective.

Direct quotations, which are usually manufactured by the editors, are one way to add some color into the copy, but they often end up full of corporate buzzwords and overused phrases. It is very common for organizations that use the informational tone in newsletters and on their intranet to receive suggestions from readers about using more photographs and graphics, or maybe even to add cartoons or crossword puzzles. These suggestions are often the reader's way of saying, "Please put some color and a little life into the publication!"

A good writer can manage to make the informational tone interesting by putting the facts in context for employees and making the messages personally relevant. But there's another problem with the informational tone: It can lack credibility because employees know organizational communications are not being written by objective third-party sources. An external press release may read "XYZ Corp. released its third-quarter earnings report today," but the use of the word "its" is awkward internally and lacks credibility. Employees know the organization's internal communication professionals are writing the materials at the behest of the organization's leaders. A statement such as "Company officials released XYZ

Corp.'s third-quarter earnings statement" or an informal statement such as "We released our third-quarter earnings report today" is much more credible.

> The informational tone is an effective tone to get information out, but it falls short of getting messages through. And ultimately, you're not really communicating if your main purpose is merely to impart information to the masses.

The informational tone is inherently detached and, therefore, doesn't lend itself well to open and honest feedback or peer-to-peer communications. While the informational tone is a solidly professional sounding tone, it does not engage employees so it will not produce the most effective communication possible. It is an effective tone to get information out, but it falls short of getting messages through. And ultimately, you're not really communicating if your main purpose is merely to impart information to the masses.

## The Partner Tone

The partner tone approaches employees as business partners and connotes a sense of "We're all in this together." It seeks to impart understanding among employees and to earn their support for the organization's strategies. The partner tone typically uses conversational language and simple words. It avoids stilted business-speak. It contains facts, but it seeks to add color and context to them. It paints pictures and has personality, sometimes a lot of personality. It is warm and it embraces storytelling as a highly effective communication technique. Those who are masters of the partner tone understand that emotion is a powerful key to communication that gets through. The partner tone doesn't masquerade as a third-party objective source. To the contrary, sometimes it proudly plays a cheerleader role. It is credible and it is authentic. In some organizations, the partner tone can work well with humor and edgy copy.

Figure 6.4 contrasts a simple e-letter signoff statement written in an information tone with the same safety sentiment written in a partner tone. The employee communicators' intent is to use the sign-off language at the end of an e-letter following a series of several organizational announcements. In this, the informational-toned signoff is professional but somewhat detached, trite and bland. The partner tone is less professional but more compelling, more inclusive and more engaging. The information tone seems to be talking to employees whereas the partner tone seems to be talking with employees. "Thanks" instead of "Thank you" is more conversational, less formal, more personal and more like the way you'd talk to your business partner. The safety line in the partner toned sign-off, taken from the 1980s TV show *Hill Street Blues*, is perhaps a little edgy, which makes it more compelling to read. The use of "let's" makes the safety message more inclusive because it is coming from a perspective of "us" rather than "you."

**Figure 6.4: Informational and Partner Tone Contrast**

| Informational Tone | Thank you for reading. Please remember to work Safely. |
|---|---|
| Partner Tone | Thanks for reading. And hey, let's be careful out there! |

The partner tone tells employees what they need to do and why they are doing it. The "why" doesn't have to be a lengthy explanation, but it should give employees some reasonable idea of why they're being asked to do something. For example, the corporate headquarters staff of a large retail chain writes an e-mail message to their store managers that reads in part: "Change all labels immediately." This directive-toned communication could be edited to a partner tone and read: "Due to changes in state regulations, you'll need to change all labels. It is important you do so right away to avoid heavy fines."

The partner tone also encourages frequent feedback from employees and it seems more authentic than the previously discussed tones because it approaches employees as partners and with a connotation of "Tell us what you think. We really do want to know." Its spirit of "We're all in this together" also encourages peer-to-peer communication aimed at continuous improvement and discovering innovative ways to solve problems.

Although it could be used in any format, a partner tone seems most conducive to digital communication channels, such as e-letters and intranets, where there isn't a longstanding tradition of other tones and, therefore, preconceived notions of what the tone should be. The tone also works well with podcasts, speeches and other spoken communications because of its conversational language. A partner tone may seem inappropriate in a print publication designed like a traditional newspaper because those publications are so identified with the informational tone. The partner tone is more compatible with a more modern magazine design where lively writing is expected.

The partner tone can be highly engaging and highly effective, but it may not be right for every organization. The organization must be committed to open and honest communications. Message credibility is crucial for a partner tone. A high degree of trust must exist between an organization's leaders and its employees. The organization must be committed to receiving feedback and facilitating peer-to-peer communications. The partner tone is not well-suited for command-and-control management styles. Newer organizations with flatter organizational structures will find such a tone easier to implement.

If an organization doesn't have open and honest communications, trust between management and employees, feedback systems and peer-to-peer communication structures, it will have a difficult time engaging employees and achieving consistent highly effective communications regardless of what tone is used. Such an organization may be able to produce consistent, clear, efficient and flawless communications, but it will never be able to engage employees fully and maximize communication effectiveness. The ill-fated CEO e-mail in Figure 6.3 could have been written in a partner tone, but it would still not have been effective because the tone would not have been aligned with the company's personality or its internal brand. The message would not have been credible because the company's "say" didn't match its "do."

## The Voice of the Brand

Perhaps the best choice to produce consistently effective communication is The Voice of the Brand because it is by definition authentic, and it allows for its tone to evolve as the organization changes. The Voice of the Brand is made up of two parts: what the organization is (about 80%) and what the organization is aspiring to be (about 20%). You can think of "what the organization is" as the organization's personality.

> The Voice of the Brand is credible because 80% of its tone is made up of what the organization actually is. But it causes slow and steady change with 20% of its tone by articulating what the organization is trying to become.

As discussed at the beginning of this chapter, the organization's personality can be derived from many factors including its type of industry, its leaders' management style, its business model, its type of employees, its history, its reputation, its formal policies and its unwritten rules. What makes the Voice of the Brand different from the organization's personality is that it is pushing and pulling the organization to achieve what it is trying to become. Change is inevitable for all organizations and most are actively engaged in trying to transform their workforce and how they do business to continue to meet the challenges they face.

The Voice of the Brand is credible because 80% of its tone is made up of what the organization actually is. But it causes slow and steady change with 20% of its tone by articulating what the organization is trying to become. For example, an organization that is trying to get its employees to break out of their silos and work together more might start referring to work groups as "teams" instead of "departments." This small wording change would be just one of many other changes all aimed at causing the workforce to change.

The Voice of the Brand is different for every organization. Each organization will have to discover its own voice and then figure out how to bring it to life.

To find the Voice of the Brand, internal communication professionals need to have a deep understanding of their organization's brand and vision. They should look at two broad areas: aspirations and inspirations.

Aspirations to examine include the organization's logo, its tagline, its marketing and advertising language, its annual report verbiage, and its mission and vision statements. Each of those areas is considered quite important so organizations invest a good deal of time, effort and money into their development to ensure they accurately reflect the organization's brand.

> To find the Voice of the Brand, look at two broad areas: aspirations and inspirations.

Inspirations can include industry and organizational pride, business drivers and anything about which people in the organization are passionate. Internal communication professionals can conduct focus groups and one-on-one interviews to understand better these inspirations. Other insights can be gained by simply observing employees in meetings, in break rooms and in interactions with one another, and by paying attention to feedback they provide on messages. These situations can help reveal what makes them proud about their profession and organization and what they are passionate about. Tapping into pride and passion is a powerful way to engage employees.

Once you begin to understand the aspirations and inspirations of your organization, you can begin to develop the Voice of the Brand and use it in every internal communication possible. It will likely take some time to understand and implement the Voice of the Brand completely, and once it is developed, it may evolve over time.

Here are some ways to bring the Voice of the Brand to life:

- **Style Guide:** Create a brand vocabulary in a style guide, such as the example shown in Chapter 3, and ensure it is used in all broad-based organizational communication.

- **Glossary:** Create a glossary of industry and organizational terms, as discussed in Chapter 3, and make sure it includes the brand vocabulary. The glossary can be made available to the entire organization.

- **Graphic Design:** Make sure the look and feel of all internal communication should reflect the organization's brand. Published branding guidelines, such as those discussed in Chapter 3, can help drive consistency.

- **Guiding Principles:** Devise guiding principles, such as those shown in Chapter 3, that codify the brand philosophy as it pertains to internal communication.

- **Leverage Media:** Use a communication matrix, such as the one detailed in Chapter 2, to think about how to articulate the Voice of the Brand in each communication channel. Look for ways to focus on the things employees are proud of and passionate about. Look for ways to model and celebrate brand behavior.

- **Feedback:** Positive and negative reactions from employees will let you know when you are on the right track as you begin to implement the Voice of the Brand. Look for messages that resonate with your organization's employees.

Figure 6.5 shows an example of a message formatted in a directive tone and contrasts the same message in a Voice of the Brand tone for a company that believes "fun" is a competitive advantage. These messages have been modified only slightly from a real life example where an internal client submitted a directive toned message that employee communicators edited to reflect the company's Voice of the Brand. Note that the directive message does not provide a contact number. The message submitter didn't want feedback and believed all the facts were presented and there wouldn't be any questions. Also note the "Thank you for your cooperation" sentence at the end. This was the message submitter's attempt to add a little warmth to the message.

**Figure 6.5: Directive Tone contrasted with fun Voice of the Brand tone**

| Directive Tone | There are 259 stores that have not yet provided us group participant information for the Santa Claus promotion. These forms were due Nov. 10. We must have them returned IMMEDIATELY! Failure to do so will result in no payment. Attached is a list of those that have complied and those that have not. Thank you for your cooperation in this matter. |
|---|---|
| Fun Voice of the Brand Tone | Making a List and Checking it Twice: 259 stores have not yet provided their group participant information for the Santa Claus promotion. They're overdue, folks, and we must have the complete information right away to pay Santa's little helpers. So, no info means no Santa Claus. Attached is a list of who's been naughty and who's been nice. Questions? Chief Elf Julie Smith has all the answers. Call her at her North Pole office, ext. 2826. |

# Chapter Conclusion

Finding the Voice of the Brand for your organization and bringing it to life can have dramatic effects on your work's credibility and authenticity, making it a powerful way to enhance your communication efforts. It can tap into the things about your organization that resonate with your employee audiences. Because it is aligned with your brand, it can help drive brand behavior. It can be liberating to you as a writer because it allows you to be inspirational and aspirational without it sounding awkward. Done correctly, it positions the communications as coming from the organization itself and not just from the management team, which makes it more inclusive. And one more thing: while the Voice of the Brand can have a dramatic effect, it doesn't cost the organization a dime.

## Chapter Exercises

1. The CEO memo shown in Figure 6.3 was not an effective means of communicating. The CEO was attempting to make some legitimate points, but the message tone was too parental and the channel choice of e-mail was not well-suited to such a difficult message. A face-to-face meeting probably would have been a better choice. Write some talking points that the CEO could have delivered at a manager meeting instead.

_____

_____

_____

_____

_____

_____

_____

_____

_____

_____

_____

_____

_____

_____

_____

_____

_____

_____

_____

_____

_____

_____

_____

_____

_____

_____

_____

## Chapter 7

# Communicating Employee Benefits

"Make it simple. Make it memorable.
Make it inviting to look at.
Make it fun to read."
– Leo Burnett

**Chapter Overview:** Whether you are a professional who specializes in employee benefits communication or you oversee a broad range of internal communications, you'll need to understand the unique aspects of employee benefits communication to maximize internal communication in your organization. Employee benefits are important to employees and their perceived value contributes to employee engagement.

In this chapter, you will learn some of the unique characteristics of employee benefits communication and discover some powerful strategies that can be used to leverage those characteristics. Those strategies can be used to formulate tactics that can be incorporated into the strategic communication planning process detailed in Chapter 5; in turn, you can use that process to formulate a comprehensive strategic employee benefits communication plan for your organization.

Employee benefits are an important part of attracting and retaining employees, and communicating those benefits effectively is another way your organization can enhance employee engagement. Several unique aspects of employee benefits communication need to be understood by internal communication professionals. Unique characteristics can be approached simply as communication challenges that need to be overcome or they can be viewed as opportunities that can be leveraged to create more effective communication strategies.

## Benefits Wide-Ranging and Complicated

Employee benefits are wide-ranging and can be quite complicated. They include healthcare plans, disability plans, dental plans, vision plans, wellness programs, 401(k) and other retirement plans, flexible spending accounts, paid time off, family and medical leave, telecommuting, training opportunities, tuition reimbursement, on-site child care, employee discounts and other special benefit offerings. An organization may have separate benefit packages for each of its unions, another package for its hourly employees, another for its salaried employees and another for its executives. Adding to the complexity, federal and state laws regulate many of these benefits and some of those laws concern how benefits are communicated. For instance, federal law requires that an organization provide employees with a detailed written Summary Plan Description (SPD) for each healthcare plan it offers (Department of Labor, 2013). The SPD must, among other things, provide a summary of coverage, steps to file a claim and the process to appeal a claim. There are always changes in laws and new legislation that necessitate benefits communication. Internal communication professionals can help employees to understand how these laws affect their benefit choices.

Many organizations offer flexible benefits that require employees to make selections from various plans. The organization will need to assist its employees by providing them with good information and analytical tools so they can make the best choices for themselves and their families. Organizations that offer flexible benefits typically have an annual open enrollment period for employees to sign up for benefits. For many organizations, open enrollment is an opportunity to build understanding and enhance the perception of their employee benefit offerings. Many organizations conduct comprehensive open enrollment communication campaigns aimed at enhancing employee understanding of their benefits package and boosting participation in benefits options.

## Influencing Perception Through Communication

An objective of employee benefits communication is to ensure that employees understand their benefits and they highly value them. Of course, when employees understand and highly value their benefits, it makes sense that they are more committed to their jobs. The perception employees have about the value of their employee benefits is often a direct result of how well the benefits offerings are communicated. In many instances, communication can be even more important than the benefit offerings themselves in shaping employee perceptions. Employees can't value benefits unless they are aware they have them and they understand their value. For example, employees in Company A with average benefits may value their benefits higher than employees in Company B even though Company B has arguably better benefits simply because Company A does a better job communicating its benefits offerings. Company A not only provides information and tools to help employees better understand their benefits, but it also markets and promotes the products and services to put them in the best possible light. Employees in Company A not only value their benefits, but they feel better about their company for providing them with what seems to be a great benefits package. Therefore, Company A may have more engaged employees despite its slightly inferior benefits.

As John Moses, Ph.D., pointed out (2011), communicators need to approach benefits communication less like educators and more like marketers. Moses says we need to shift from just educating employees about their benefits to motivating employees to use them. Figure 7.1 shows the communication mix that Moses suggests.

**Figure 7.1: Benefits Communication Mix**

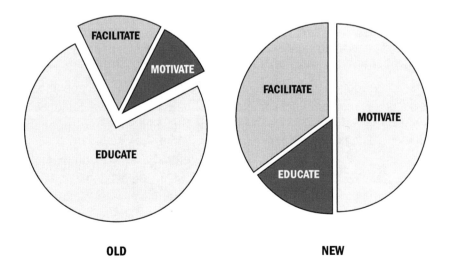

OLD                                                        NEW

Using a marketing approach in the manner Moses suggests can positively affect employee perceptions of employee benefits. For instance, most large organizations have employee discounts on things such as cell phone plans, computers, dry cleaning, homeowner and car insurance, movie tickets and tickets to sports events. Although such discounts are often quite popular with employees, many organizations don't do much to promote or position them in a manner that gives the organization credit for providing them. Often a company already supplying a product or service for an organization also will offer an employee discount on its products or services through e-mails and fliers sent to employees. Usually a standard 10% discount is offered to employees by organizations the company works with. But some organizations aggressively negotiate employee discounts, which they see as a way to attract, retain and reward employees. These organizations market these discounts as, "We have negotiated these deals for you," thus giving them credit for helping their employees enjoy discounts for products and services. Organizations are able to negotiate such deals because they have a large number of employees they can steer toward a particular vendor.

In some cases, employees may not actually even use a particular benefit offered by their organization, but the employees may have an enhanced perception of their organization simply because the organization provides benefits such as tuition reimbursement for continuing education, discounts on health club memberships or cash to those adopting a child. These benefits reflect how the organization values its employees.

Figure 7.2 shows how employees rank employee benefits based on their perceptions of their package's value. Obviously the best-case scenario, which is to have great benefits and to communicate them well, ranks as No. 1, and the worst-case scenario, which is to have inferior benefits and communicate them poorly, ranks No. 4. The interesting aspect is how employees rank inferior benefits higher if they are communicated well (ranking No. 2) and underrate good benefits if they are communicated poorly (ranking No. 3). As in many aspects of life, perception is reality.

**Figure 7.2: Perception Ranking of Employee Benefits**

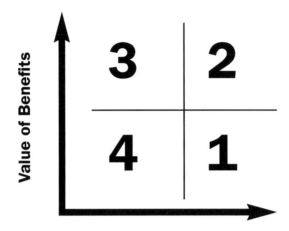

**Effectiveness of Benefit Communication**

# Determining Who Communicates Benefit Information

In some organizations, the internal communication professionals partner with the benefits team to communicate benefit information. Because benefit information can be complex and unique, some organizations will choose to have a professional communicator, who is well-versed in benefit communication, dedicated to the task. Other organizations will allow their benefits team to handle the communications themselves or have them outsource some or all of the communications to employee benefits consultants. The third-party vendors who administer the benefit plans also provide many communications to employees. These will be discussed in more detail later in this chapter. Communications are often handled by a combination of internal and external sources.

Regardless of who handles it, all employee benefits communication should be aligned with the organization's business objectives and communication strategies to achieve maximum effectiveness.

# Understanding the Unique Aspects of Employee Benefits

The basic principles of internal communication apply to communicating employee benefits as well, but internal communication professionals should be aware of some unique aspects of employee benefits communication. Here are five important ways that employee benefits communication is different from other forms of internal communication:

- Benefits are more personal than workplace information and may involve families.

- Spouses often are the decision-makers in making benefit selections.

- Benefits communication usually involves many outside vendors, each of which provides communication about its plans and services.

- Employees typically don't care much about benefits until they need them.

- Benefits information is specialized, complicated and different than information about the business.

Let's look at each unique characteristic more closely and list some possible strategies and potential tactics an organization could use to communicate employee benefits more effectively.

**Benefits are Personal.** Employee benefits hit home and, therefore, are much more personal to employees than information about the workplace. Benefits involve not only employees, but also their spouses and children. A strategy might be to make employee benefits communication as personally relevant as possible. Here are some potential tactics to support that strategy:

- All benefits communication must answer this basic employee question: What's in it for me and my family?

- Examples that individuals can relate to should be used in benefit communication. Figure 7.2 shows how examples of other people can help an employee decide which healthcare plan to choose.

- Avoid benefits jargon and acronyms. STD clearly refers to Short-Term Disability to employee benefit professionals, but the acronym means Sexually Transmitted Disease to almost everyone else. 401(k) refers to the IRS tax code that governs such plans, but calling it a "Savings Plan" or even a "401(k) Savings Plan" is probably more appealing to employees than a "401(k) Plan."

- When technical terms have to be used, define them. Create a benefits wiki on the organization's intranet that defines terms that employees may encounter.

- Personal and family settings should be depicted in photographs and videos. Creating these images can be especially helpful for employees who are from cultures where family needs are considered more important than individual autonomy.

- Produce employee benefit materials that can be taken home. Open enrollment materials, for instance, will likely be read at the kitchen table. Print is still an effective medium for complex materials that need to be taken home and studied.

- Allow employee benefit websites to be accessed from home and optimize them for mobile devices.

- Develop an employee benefit smartphone app that provides personalized information.

- Produce personally customized materials whenever possible. For instance, many organizations produce an annual benefits statement that includes employee-specific information—how much money an employee has saved in his or her 401(k) plan, how much the organization contributes to the individual's healthcare coverage, how much the employee has received in tuition reimbursement, etc.

- Be aware of differences in benefit offerings for part-time employees, international employees, union members, etc.

- Provide personal modeling. For instance, some organizations make an online 401(k) calculator available that allows employees to plug in numbers to see how much money they can save for retirement by changing the percentage of their monthly contribution. Employees enter information about their ages, how many years they plan to work, their salaries, what percentage of their salaries they are contributing, etc. to get a customized savings plan.

- Provide lifecycle modeling. For instance, show how typical employees would select 401(k) investments based on where they are in the lifecycle: younger investors would assume more risk for possible higher returns while those nearing retirement would take on less risk in favor of stability.

- Provide comparison charts to help employees easily see the differences between healthcare plans and make better choices.

- Provide employees with a personalized medical plan worksheet that uses actual claims data from previous years to project individual costs under each medical plan option.

- Allow employees to share wellness tips with one another through internal social media sites.

**Figure 7.3: Personalizing Benefits Selection**

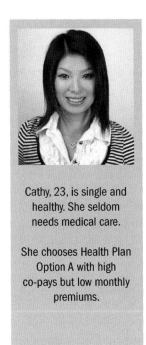

Cathy, 23, is single and healthy. She seldom needs medical care.

She chooses Health Plan Option A with high co-pays but low monthly premiums.

Rick, 40, and his wife just had a new baby girl.

He chooses Health Plan B for complete coverage for his family. It has moderate co-pays and moderate monthly premiums.

Hank, 58, is married and has Type 1 diabetes.

He chooses Health Plan C that provides comprehensive coverage for his medications and needed supplies. It has low co-pays but high-monthly premiums.

**Spouses are an Audience.** In many cases, employee spouses may be the decision-makers who decide which employee benefit plans to select. A strategy might be to consider employee spouses as a key audience for some employee benefits communication, such as open enrollment materials. All of the potential tactics listed under the previous strategy are applicable to this strategy as well. Here are some additional tactics that could be used to support the spousal communication strategy:

- Copy and scripts should refer to "you and your family" and should be written in such a manner that they could be clearly understood by employee spouses.

- Mail open enrollment and other relevant employee benefits communication to employee homes.

- Invite employees and their spouses to open enrollment meetings or employee benefit fairs where they can meet and talk directly to benefits provider representatives. Hold the fairs during hours that spouses can attend.

> Employee spouses may be the decision-makers who decide which employee benefit plans to select.

**Coordinating Vendor Communications.** Most organizations provide many of their employee benefits through a myriad of third-party vendors. Large healthcare provider companies such as United Healthcare, WellPoint and Kaiser Permanente administer healthcare plans. Large financial institutions such as Fidelity Investments, Vanguard and American Century administer 401(k) savings plans. These employee benefit plan vendors typically send a large amount of communication to employees to inform them about their products and services. Often, the initial contract that established the relationship with the vendor included provisions for communication and sometimes for educational workshops. Sometimes each vendor provides a customized website for the organization. Typically, vendors devise their own communication plans. A strategy might be to coordinate the various vendor communications. Here are some possible tactics to support such a strategy:

- Create a communication calendar and work with vendors on the content and timing of their communications. Know what messages they are sending and when they are sending them. Ensure that key messages the vendors are sending aren't in conflict with broader organizational messaging and ensure that the timing of the vendor communications doesn't conflict with other organizational communications.

- Provide vendors with broad organizational messaging and encourage them to incorporate key messaging into their materials when appropriate. (Note: Many vendors use standard language for all the organizations they provide benefits for and they may not be able to make any copy changes. But in some cases, they may be able to change headings.)

- Provide vendors with organizational style guides, graphic standards, logos and photographs. They may be willing to incorporate the organization's branded look and feel into the design of their communications and website landing pages. (Note: Many vendors use template designs and can't make any changes. But in some cases, they may be able to change colors to the organization's colors.)

- Consolidate links from the organization's intranet to the various vendor websites.

- Review vendor websites that have been customized for the organization. Check for consistency with organizational messages and organizational branding.

**Making Benefits Information Available on Demand.** Employees typically look closely at their benefits when they are first hired and then don't pay much attention to them until they have a life changing event—they get married, they have a child, they adopt a child, they get divorced, they or family members are diagnosed with a serious illness or disability, they become disabled, a family member dies, they decide to pursue a higher education degree, they are nearing retirement, their children are entering college, etc. Employees often go from caring little about benefits to caring greatly about them as soon as they experience a life change event. A strategy might be to make benefits information available on demand. Some potential tactics that could support that strategy might include:

- Make sure all benefit plan information is available online, is searchable and is available from home computers and portable devices. Summary Plan Descriptions are cumbersome to read, but they become much more useful if they are online and searchable.

- Create a Benefit Solution Center phone line where employees can ask questions and get answers within 24 hours.

- Make sure all recruiting and new hire communications contain appropriate benefits information.

- Create life change kits and websites categorized by major life change events.

- Proactively seek out employees who are experiencing life change events and provide them with appropriate information. For instance, employees who are nearing retirement could be identified and invited to participate in retirement planning workshops.

**Using Experts to Communicate.** Employees generally cite their immediate supervisor as their preferred choice to receive internal communication, but that is not necessarily the case for employee benefits information. Benefits information is specialized, complicated and different than information about the business so employees want to hear information about benefit plans from those who are experts in the field. A strategy might be to use the organization and vendor's experts to communicate complex benefits information. Potential tactics to support that strategy might include:

- Hold brown bag lunches on a weekly basis with internal benefits experts or vendor representatives to talk about a variety of topics such as the Affordable Care Act, retirement planning, continuing education and tuition reimbursement or health and wellness issues.

- Write blogs or record podcasts or video blogs with internal benefits experts or vendor representatives speaking on a variety of benefits-related topics.

- Review vendor contracts to make sure all the agreed upon communication and educational opportunities are being utilized. Vendor contracts often outline a specific and committed number of hours the vendor will spend educating employees or a specific dollar amount they will spend on communications. Sometimes, if a vendor has been a long-time provider, those commitments fall by the wayside and are forgotten.

# Chapter Conclusion

An organization's overall messages and its employee benefits messages can enhance one another if the link between them is shown. In contrast, if benefits messages are seen as being disconnected from the organization's vision, they won't be taken nearly as seriously as they would otherwise so employees will be less likely to get on board with any changes being asked of them. By showing these connections, you can help employees see how their individual efforts contribute to the overall goals, thereby enhancing employee engagement.

Employee benefits and other human resource communication will be more effective if aligned to the organization's vision. A benefits message, particularly one aimed at changing employee behavior, will be seen as more credible if it is viewed as being directly tied to the organization's larger organizational strategies, business objectives or change efforts. For instance, let's say one of the key messages coming from ABC Company's leaders is that the company needs to do more to control costs. A number of business initiatives are already underway aimed at cutting waste and costs. The ABC Benefits department is supporting the company's efforts by seeking to control healthcare costs, which cost the company millions a year. The company can save money if employees choose the healthcare plans best suited for them, choose less expensive generic prescription drugs, and participate in the company's wellness programs, thereby enjoying healthier lives so they don't get sick as often.

## Chapter Exercises

1. The XYZ Corporation has decided to leverage better its employee discounts to help attract and retain employees, and to enhance employee perceptions about the value of their employee benefits package. One of the tactics they have come up with is to consolidate all of the employee discounts on one webpage with links to each of the vendors that provides them. Devise some other tactics they could use. How can the company position the information so it gets the credit for providing the discount instead of the vendor?

_____

_____

_____

_____

_____

_____

_____

_____

_____

2. List some ways internal social media tools can be used to communicate employee benefits information.

_____

_____

_____

_____

_____

_____

_____

_____

_____

## Chapter References

Department of Labor, "Health Plans and Benefits" retrieved July 30, 2013, from http://www.dol.gov/dol/topic/health-plans/planinformation.htm

Moses, J. (2011). "Benefits Communication Is So 1980s … Market Your Benefits and Thrive!" _Benefits Quarterly,_ 27(2), 28-33.

# Chapter 8

# Communicating with Employees During a Crisis

*"Let our advance worrying become advance thinking and planning."*
*– Winston Churchill*

**Chapter Overview:** Every organization should have a crisis communication plan that includes effective internal communication as a way to help the organization recover as fully and quickly as possible and to help it protect its brand image from the inside out.

I n this chapter, you'll learn about the vital role internal communication can play during a crisis, and how a well-prepared organization can emerge from a crisis with an even stronger brand image and even greater commitment from its employees.

A crisis can strike any organization at any time. A crisis could range from a minor incident that disrupts an organization's operations to a catastrophic event that causes an organization to cease to exist. Crisis situations can involve the health and safety of employees, customers and the community, and they could affect an organization's financial stability, legal liability and public image. Personal scandals, workplace violence, embarrassing viral videos, natural disasters, manmade disasters and infectious diseases are just some of the crises any organization might face.

The primary concern for an organization isn't whether a crisis will strike, but rather how prepared the organization is to manage the inevitable crisis when it unexpectedly occurs. Being able to manage a crisis is critical for every organization and doing so takes effective communication internally and externally. Every organization should have a detailed crisis communication plan to help it respond appropriately and quickly, and every crisis communication plan should include a well thought-out internal communication plan. Many organizations have crisis communication plans that are woefully outdated and others have no written plans at all. These are communication failures waiting to happen.

Many organizations that suddenly find themselves in a crisis situation become immediately concerned about the potential damage to their public image, and as a result, they tend to focus externally on the news media and increasingly more on social media channels. But enlightened organizations know their employee audience is just as important as their external audiences because employees are directly involved in the crisis recovery efforts and because, as discussed in Chapter 1, employees serving as brand ambassadors can affect an organization's public image as well. Employees expect to hear open and honest communication from their organization during a crisis. Organizations need the full support of their employees to recover from a crisis as fully and as quickly as possible.

## Realizing the Positive Effects of Internal Communication During a Crisis

Crisis communication is the lifeblood of crisis management (Coombs, 2011). Ineffective internal communication during a crisis situation potentially can spell outright doom for an organization. Confused employees can't respond to the crisis or to customers properly. Irreparable damage can be done to a brand. On the other hand, effective internal communication during a crisis can have many positive effects. Effective internal communication:

- Results in clear, concise, timely, accurate and consistent employee messaging that can help ensure an appropriate and quick response to a crisis, and reduce or eliminate rumors and false information.

- Saves an organization time and money by helping employees eliminate mistakes and inefficiencies in their recovery efforts.

- Allows employees to know how well their organization is responding to a crisis, which enhances credibility and trust in the organization.

- Affects employee perceptions about the organization and thus affects motivation and long-term employee engagement.

- Motivates employees to act as Brand Champions in their interactions with customers as well as their families, friends and others in the community, which helps protect an organization's public image.

## Approaching with Anticipate, Prepare, Practice

One approach to crisis management is what risk management expert Vincent Covello, Ph.D., calls APP—Anticipate, Prepare and Practice (2011). This approach calls for anticipating the most likely crisis scenarios, preparing for them by gathering information, and then planning appropriate responses. Internal communication professionals can take Covello's APP approach and apply it to the employee portion of a crisis communication plan. Let's look at each of those areas from an internal communication perspective.

## Anticipating

Working with their external communication counterparts, internal communication professionals should help to identify the five most likely crisis scenarios with which their particular organization could be faced. Of course, an organization can't anticipate every potential crisis situation, but the information prepared for the top five most likely scenarios and the process of gathering that information will be useful no matter what crisis strikes.

What the top five most likely scenarios are will depend in part on the organization's type of industry. For instance, an airline would be most concerned with a plane crash, an electrical utility would be most concerned with a massive power outage and an oil company would be most concerned with some type of environmental disaster. The internal communication professionals will want to think through the most likely crisis scenarios and see them through their employees' eyes. They also will want to identify potential crisis situations that involve the employees themselves, such as work-related deaths or serious on-the-job injuries, union strikes, massive layoffs or major organizational restructurings.

## Preparing

It is best to be prepared as much as possible before a crisis strikes. An organization that hasn't prepared for crisis communication can become overwhelmed quickly. There is simply too much happening too fast. Communication failures can compound a situation by adding a communication crisis on top of the initial crisis. On the other hand, preparation can result in faster response times and better quality responses. A well-prepared organization with effective communication can emerge from a crisis with an even stronger brand image in the minds of the public and its employees.

Time is of the essence in a crisis situation. By having information pre-gathered and processes pre-determined, you will be able to send crisis responses out more quickly. With the 24-hour news cycle and the prevalence of social media in the workplace, employees may hear about a crisis situation from an external source first. False information and rumors will spread quickly. It is important for an organization to respond as soon as possible and establish itself as the most trusted source for information about the crisis. Otherwise, employees, just like the public, will turn to other sources for information, and those sources may not be telling the story the organization wants told.

> A well-prepared organization with effective communication can emerge from a crisis with an even stronger brand image in the minds of the public and its employees.

Proper preparation allows messages to be sent quicker, and it also can enhance the quality of the response. It is difficult to think clearly and prioritize in the midst of a crisis with the clock ticking. Taking the time to pre-gather materials under calm circumstances and carefully thinking through all the processes that need to be executed to send messages will ensure a better quality response. Communicators can take the time to work with the organization's leaders, safety team and legal counsel to fine-tune messages, and they can work with IT departments to establish emergency communication channels and back-up systems.

**What to Prepare:** Exactly what to prepare will vary from one organization to another. But some common components that should be part of any organization's crisis communication plan for employees include the following:

1. Emergency notification system and contact information.
2. Roles and responsibilities for crisis communication team members.
3. Key messaging for likely crisis scenarios.
4. A crisis communication policy for employees that determines who can talk to the news media and who can post to social media sites.
5. An initial employee update template.
6. A list of grief counselors who can be called upon to assist employees.
7. A Communication Channel Matrix.
8. A list of places for employees to donate.
9. A post-crisis evaluation form.

Let's look at each of these areas in more detail.

**1. Emergency Notification System and Contact Information:** It is crucial for an organization to contact employees who need to respond quickly to a crisis. Many organizations have sophisticated automated emergency notification systems that simultaneously send alerts via text message, e-mail and phone and keep on sending them until employees respond. Other organizations set up text message and e-mail distribution lists and manual phone trees. Whichever system an organization chooses, accurate and up-to-date contact information is the key to its success.

**2. Roles and Responsibilities:** A communication team will react more smoothly under the stress of a crisis situation if roles and responsibilities have been established and clearly communicated ahead of time. They should be contained in a written crisis communication manual, and they should specify who will draft, fact-check, approve and send messages, who will monitor feedback, and who will serve as liaison with the rest of the crisis management team.

**3. Key Messaging for Likely Scenarios:** Once likely scenarios have been developed for the larger crisis communication plan, an organization's employee communicators should establish key messages for employees. That messaging undoubtedly will be based on the messages created for the news media and other external audiences. It is the responsibility of internal communication professionals to think through those external messages from the employees' perspective. What will employee concerns be? What information will employees need to know?

Internal communication in a crisis situation should focus first on the well-being of employees, and then on how employees can help the organization to recover and how they can help protect the organization's brand image. Employees, like all audiences, will need to know you care before they will care what you know. To have the most impact, Covello (2011) says crisis messaging should include compassion, conviction and optimism.

The sample messages in Figure 8.1 were created using Covello's compassion, conviction and optimism approach.

**Figure 8.1: Sample Crisis Communication Key Messages**

| **Message No. 1:** Our immediate concern is for the safety and well-being of all of our employees. | **Message No. 2:** We will find out what caused this terrible accident and take appropriate action. | **Message No. 3:** We are committed to doing the right thing. |
|---|---|---|
| **Supporting Message:** We are closely monitoring the status of the injured employees and offering support to them and their families. | **Supporting Message:** Many questions are unanswered at this early stage and we do not want to speculate, but we will get to the bottom of this and find out what caused this terrible accident. | **Supporting Message:** Regardless of costs, we will do whatever is necessary to ensure the safety of all our employees. |
| **Supporting Message:** We have set up a hotline for families to call to make sure their loved one is OK. | **Supporting Message:** We are cooperating fully with investigators to determine what caused this terrible accident. | **Supporting Message:** Working together, we will get through this difficult time. |
| **Supporting Message:** We are offering free counseling services for all employees as they deal with this terrible tragedy. | **Supporting Message:** We will take all necessary steps to ensure this never happens again. | **Supporting Message:** We will answer all of your questions, and we will keep you updated on any developments. |

Here are some other risk management communication suggestions from Covello (2011 and 2003) that are appropriate for employee crisis messaging as well:

- Focus more on what you are doing than on what you aren't doing.

- Primacy/Recency: During a crisis, people remember the first thing and the last thing you tell them the most.

- 1N=3P: It takes three positive things to make up for one negative thing. Balance bad news with good news.

- AGL-4: During a crisis, people's intellect is reduced four grade levels from the highest level they achieved. Therefore, craft your messaging in clear, concise and simple terms.

> Employees need to know you care before they will care what you know.

- Avoid using distant, abstract, unfeeling language when discussing harm, deaths, injuries and illnesses.

- Disclose risk information as soon as possible; fill information vacuums.

- If information is evolving or incomplete, emphasize appropriate reservations about its reliability.

- If in doubt, lean toward sharing more information, not less or (employees) may think something significant is being hidden or withheld.

- If you don't know or are unsure about an answer, express willingness to get back to the questioner with a response by an agreed-upon deadline. Do not speculate.

**4. Communication Policy for Employees:** Internal communication professionals should work with their legal teams to draft a communication policy for employees to follow regarding their interactions with the news media, on social media channels and with other external outlets such as letters to the editor in a newspaper or as a caller to a radio talk show. A communication policy is, of course, in effect all the time, but it becomes especially important during a crisis situation so I am including it in this listing of crisis communication tools.

Traditionally, especially during a crisis, organizations have tried to control their messaging closely by channeling all external communication through a trained spokesperson who provides the key messaging. However, with so many external communication outlets available to employees, this is becoming more difficult to enforce. Employees often want to defend their organizations or correct false or misleading information they hear or see.

This is especially true during crisis situations when situations are developing quickly and information is being spread rapidly. In fact, some organizations want their employees to participate in social media channels and other external outlets to add credible and informed voices to the discussion. Some organizations will even allow their employees to do interviews with news media as long as the employees only talk about areas with which they work directly and they refer all other questions to the organization's official spokesperson. Other organizations provide training for selected employees who can then be called upon to be employee spokespersons. Employees may add expertise and credibility.

Figure 8.2 contains communication guidelines for employees from the fictitious XYZ Corporation. These guidelines have been adapted from some I wrote for an actual organization. They are presented here as an example of a policy that subtly acknowledges there are so many social media platforms and other external outlets available that it is virtually impossible to keep employees from communicating about their organizations. Rather than prohibiting employees from talking about their organizations, these guidelines aim to help them communicate responsibly.

## Figure 8.2: XYZ Corporation Communication Guidelines for Employees

XYZ Corporation employees should be mindful of communicating information about the company in all mediums, particularly those directed to broad external audiences such as letters to the editor, radio talk shows, blog comments and social media channels. To ensure employees are able to engage in appropriate public commentary and engage in social media channels, employees should familiarize themselves with and adhere to the following guidelines:

1. Know and follow the E-Mail and Other Electronic and Telephonic Communication Systems (ETCS) Policy.

2. XYZ Corporation employees are personally responsible for the content they publish on user-generated media. Be mindful that what you publish is public for a long time—protect your privacy.

3. Make it clear you are speaking for yourself and not on behalf of XYZ Corporation.

4. If you publish content to any website outside of XYZ Corporation and it has something to do with work you do or subjects associated with XYZ Corporation, use a disclaimer such as this: "The postings on this site are my own and don't necessarily represent XYZ Corporation's positions, strategies or opinions."

5. Respect copyright, fair use and financial disclosure laws.

6. Don't provide XYZ Corporation or another's confidential or other proprietary information. Ask permission to publish or report on conversations meant to be private or internal. You must make sure you do not disclose or use confidential or proprietary information or that of any other person or company. For example, ask permission before posting someone's picture in a social network or publishing in a blog a conversation that was meant to be private.

7. You must not comment on confidential financial information such as XYZ Corporation's future business performance, business plans or prospects anywhere in the world. This includes statements about an upcoming quarter or future periods or information about alliances, and applies to anyone, including conversations with Wall Street analysts, press or other third parties (including friends). XYZ Corporation policy is not to comment on rumors in any way. You should merely say, "No comment" to rumors. Do not deny or affirm them or suggest either denial or affirmation in subtle ways.

8. Don't cite or reference clients, partners or suppliers without their approval. When you do make a reference, where possible, link back to the source.

9. Respect your audience. Don't use ethnic slurs, personal insults, obscenity, or engage in any conduct that would not be acceptable in XYZ Corporation's workplace. You also should show proper consideration for others' privacy and for topics that may be considered objectionable or inflammatory—such as politics and religion.

10. Be aware of your association with XYZ Corporation in online social networks. If you identify yourself as an XYZ Corporation employee, ensure your profile and related content is consistent with how you wish to present yourself with colleagues and clients.

11. Only those officially designated by XYZ Corporation have the authorization to speak on the company's behalf. Direct all news media inquiries to corporate communication.

12. Use good judgment. If you're about to publish something that makes you even the slightest bit uncomfortable, review the suggestions above and think about why you feel that way. Ultimately, however, you have sole responsibility for what you post or publish in any form of online social media.

13. You should make sure your online activities do not interfere with your job or commitments to customers.

**5. Initial Employee Update Template:** As mentioned previously, time is of the essence in a crisis situation, so organizations need to get out in front of the news and establish themselves as soon as possible as the most accurate and credible source of information about the situation. Having a carefully crafted employee message that can be easily adapted for a particular situation and sent out quickly will help an organization achieve this goal. Figure 8.3 shows a sample template message that could be prepared in advance and adapted when needed. It is important to label all template messaging with "THIS IS A DRILL" so a template message left on a laser printer, a copy machine, a recycle bin or somewhere else doesn't inadvertently cause confusion or panic.

**Figure 8.3: Sample Internal Communication Crisis Message Template**

**THIS IS A DRILL. THIS IS A DRILL. THIS IS A DRILL.**

Employee Update E-mail #1

To All XYZ Corp. Employees,

It is with great sadness that we are making you aware of a tragic accident that occurred at our company a short while ago. While we don't have all of the details yet, here is what we know: [INSERT BRIEF FACTS OF THE SITUATION]. The company will post information for you on its intranet and issue appropriate public statements as we confirm information.

We're working hard to get information out as fast as possible. However, it may take time to verify facts. It is important that we do not speculate and that all information we provide is accurate. Please don't spread rumors or speculate. We will continue to provide you updates as events warrant. In the meantime, you may ask questions by replying to this e-mail and we will respond as quickly as possible.

The situation is under control and we are confident no further safety risks exist. Please use your cell phones to let your family members know you are OK. They will appreciate hearing from you and this will help to keep our company phone lines open.

We are cooperating fully with authorities, and we are committed to finding out exactly what happened. We will take all necessary steps to ensure this situation never happens again.

If representatives of the news media approach you, please direct all inquiries to [INSERT NAME OF WHO IS HANDLING MEDIA INQUIRIES; PROVIDE CONTACT INFORMATION]. As a reminder, here is a link to our communication policy for employees regarding social media channels and other external outlets.

We have an obligation to our customers to continue operating our business. Please continue to focus on your job during this difficult time. Together, we will get through this terrible tragedy. Thank you.

**6. Grief Counselors:** Many organizations have an Employee Assistance Program (EAP) already in place for employees in times of need. EAP programs usually are administered by the organization's human resources team and offer free counseling for employees who may be stressed at work, have problems at home or suffer from other personal issues. These counselors, or others like them, can be called upon to offer on-site grief counseling for employees during a crisis. Employees may be experiencing a wide range of emotions during a crisis from the shock of the crisis event or from working long hours as part of the recovery effort.

It is important for organizations to demonstrate concern for their employees during a crisis. Not all employees will use the counseling services, but most employees will have an enhanced perception of their organization from just knowing the organization showed its concern for employees and took this step.

> Time is of the essence in a crisis situation, so organizations need to get out in front of the news and establish themselves as soon as possible as the most accurate and credible source of information about the situation.

**7. Crisis Communication Matrix:** A Communication Channel Matrix such as the one described in Chapter 4 can be helpful in a crisis to help determine how best to reach employees. Because communications will need to be sent as fast as possible, e-mail and text messaging are likely channels to be used for notification purposes. They are also good channels to reach employees after hours and on weekends and holidays. Employee communicators will want to examine each channel with the most likely crisis scenarios in mind.

**8. Employee Outreach:** In the aftermath of a crisis, employees often want to help the victims. A common reaction from employees is to want to send canned goods and clothing to disaster victims when money is a more effective means of getting them help. Recognizing this need and having a ready list of local blood banks and appropriate relief organizations such as the Red Cross prepared will allow this information to be sent out quickly and facilitate appropriate help.

**9. Post-Crisis Evaluation:** Following a major crisis, the larger crisis communication team should perform a post-mortem to determine what went wrong and what worked well. The internal communication professionals should contribute by focusing on the internal communication aspects of the crisis communication. Some of the questions they might raise could include the following:

- What concerns did employees have that weren't anticipated? How can these concerns be addressed in case a similar situation occurs in the future?

- What rumors or misinformation was circulated? What was the source, rumor or cause of the misinformation? Was it quelled or corrected?

- Did employees rally to support the organization? Did employees understand the situation and what they needed to do to help in the recovery efforts?

- What did employees do to help the organization's public image?

- What perceptions do employees have about the organization's handling of the crisis? Are they proud of the organization?

- Are employees going to be recognized in any way for their hard work in the recovery efforts? Were there any individual employee heroes who should be recognized? Given that employees read and hear the news and participate in social media channels, is there a place to recognize employees in external messaging?

# Practicing

Perhaps Covello's APP approach should have been APPPP for Anticipate, Prepare and Practice, Practice, Practice because the best way to be prepared for a crisis is to conduct extensive drills several times a year. It is important to practice the communication responses to the various crisis scenarios to make the crisis team better prepared at knowing what to do and when to do it. Practicing helps to uncover things in the plan that need to be changed or revised. Organizations often conduct an announced drill allowing everyone to walk through his or her duties, and then later in the year, the organization conducts an unannounced drill to test how quickly everyone is able to respond.

In addition to the crisis team's exercises, the internal communication professionals may want to conduct their own drills on their unique pieces of the response. The plan should be carried out as far as possible. For instance, actually calling the phone numbers will ensure they are accurate and reveal how likely it is that everyone can be contacted in a timely manner. The caller will simply need to state, "We're conducting a crisis communication drill. In the event of an actual emergency, we would be calling this number to inform you. Is this the best number for us to call? What is the best number to call after business hours or on weekends?"

As mentioned previously in this chapter, the crisis team should take great care clearly and prominently to mark everything in writing as "THIS IS A DRILL" in case unintended recipients see any crisis messaging.

Practice and experience will help a team perform well during a crisis. While certainly no one ever wants an actual crisis to occur, a communication team reacting to an emergency situation like a well-oiled machine is a thing of beauty that clearly demonstrates to an organization's leadership the value of effective communication.

## Further Reading

This chapter is intended to present information about crisis communication from an internal communication perspective. It is recommended that communication professionals read additional materials to get a full perspective on this important subject. Many reading materials are available for free from the Center for Risk Communication, founded by the aforementioned Dr. Vincent Covello, on the center's website: http://centerforriskcommunication.org/

In addition, the following is a suggested reading list:

Coombs, W. T., & Holladay, S. J. (Eds.). (2011). *The Handbook of Crisis Communication* (Vol. 22). John Wiley & Sons.

Coombs, W. T. (2011). *Ongoing Crisis Communication: Planning, Managing, and Responding.* Sage Publications.

Covello, V. T. (2003). "Best Practices in Public Health Risk and Crisis Communication." *Journal of Health Communication*, 85.

Covello, V. T., & Allen, F. W. (1988). *Seven Cardinal Rules of Risk Communication*. US Environmental Protection Agency.

Schultz, F., Utz, S., & Göritz, A. (2011). "Is the medium the message? Perceptions of and reactions to crisis communication via Twitter, blogs and traditional media." *Public Relations Review*, 37(1), 20-27.

Seeger, M. W. (2006). "Best practices in crisis communication: An expert panel process." *Journal of Applied Communication Research*, 34(3), 232-244.

## Chapter Conclusion

Being as prepared as possible for the inevitable crisis is critical to maximizing internal communication, and it is a great way to position you as a strategic communicator and executive counselor. Nothing builds credibility and trust in you as a professional communicator more quickly than a well-orchestrated and well-executed response to a crisis. Your executive team, key internal clients and employees are counting on you. Be ready.

## Chapter Exercises

1. The Digital Age affords us great communication channels that can reach a broad audience in an instant. But what happens when there is no electricity for an extended period of time? Brainstorm some ways you could communicate with employees who are without electricity. How could you get information to them?

_____

_____

_____

2. You are the Director of Internal Communication for a large retail company. You've just learned there has been a major collapse of shelving at your main distribution center. More than 150,000 pounds of product spilled in the collapse. Fortunately, no one was injured, but it could take weeks to sort through all the product and get it ready to go again. There will be major disruptions in the supply chain. Employees will have to work round the clock. In addition, no one knows yet why the shelving collapsed or whether shelving at other facilities is safe. Using this information, write an initial message to distribution center employees about the incident.

_____

_____

_____

## Chapter References

Coombs, W. T. (2011). *Ongoing Crisis Communication: Planning, Managing, and Responding.* Sage Publications.

Covello, V. T. (2011). "Risk Communication, Radiation, and Radiological Emergencies: Strategies, Tools, and Techniques." *Health Physics.* 101(5), 511-530.

Covello, V. T. (2003). "Best Practices in Public Health Risk and Crisis Communication." *Journal of Health Communication,* 85.

# Chapter 9

# Communicating Change to Employees

"Don't hide your strategy under a bushel.
Communicate it throughout your company.
It's better today to disclose too much than too little."
– Joel E. Ross

**Chapter Overview:** Internal communication is critical to successful change. When it's done well, internal communication not only can help your organization to manage change more effectively, but it can help your organization's executive team to lead the change it is trying to accomplish.

In this chapter, you'll learn how to make the case for change, create a sense of urgency, devise a change vision, communicate a change vision, help keep momentum going and seek to embed the change in all your internal communication efforts for enduring results.

Organizations are constantly trying to adapt to change. Sometimes external forces such as consumer behavior, the competitive environment, economic conditions, technology or legislation drive the changes. Other times, internal forces such as leadership changes, mergers, acquisitions or a desire to improve quality or productivity drive the changes. Many organizations react to or initiate change by launching large-scale initiatives designed to transform the way they operate and the way their employees do their work.

Whether an organization's efforts to enact a change succeed, and to what degree, often depends on how well the organization's efforts to change are communicated and how engaged employees are in the vision the organization is trying to achieve. Put simply, employees won't support a change they don't understand and in which they aren't in some way vested. And without employee support, a change effort is dead on arrival. On the other hand, highly engaged employees can help a change effort to succeed by maintaining productivity levels during the change, increasing the implementation time of the change, and embracing, championing and modeling the new way in which to work.

Some organizational leaders make the mistake of believing that employees will adopt change readily if it is a positive one. But all change requires adaptation. Growth in an organization is a good thing, but the truth is growth and comfort do not co-exist with one another. Another mistake leaders make is assuming that employees will embrace change and new ways to do their work simply because management says so. This assumption is true to an extent, but effective communication can help maintain productivity levels, increase implementation time and allow the change to be more successful.

The more employees understand where their organization is trying to go and what business strategies it is using to get there, the more likely they will understand how their role can contribute to the organization's success (D'Aprix, 1996). Communication plays a critical role in persuading employees to support and work toward the organization's success. Poor communication confuses employees, makes them skeptical and cynical, worsens their fears and makes them more resistant to change.

## Understanding the Eight Steps to Change

Many approaches to implementing change have been introduced over the years, and all of them call for internal communication to be a critical part of the process. One of the most successful models to implementing change is an eight-step process devised by John Kotter, Ph.D. (2002). Kotter believes these eight steps must be implemented fully and consecutively for a change effort to have the best chance for success. Figure 9.1 shows Kotter's eight steps and contains a brief description of how internal communication may play a part in implementing each step.

Let's look at each step in more detail and examine ways you can contribute to the successful implementation of each of the eight steps.

**Figure 9.1 Internal Communication Role in Change**

| STEPS TO CHANGE | INTERNAL COMMUNICATION ROLE |
|---|---|
| 1. Create a Sense of Urgency | Produce communications. |
| 2. Create a Guiding Coalition | Serve on team or act as resource. Communicate team credibility. |
| 3. Develop a Change Vision | Help draft vision and help create ways to accomplish it. |
| 4. Communicate the Vision | Create and implement communication plan. |
| 5. Empower Broad-Based Power | Communicate progress, further establish credibility of task team and remove communication barriers. |
| 6. Generate Short-Term Wins | Communicate success. |
| 7. Never Let Up | Create "evergreen" communications. |
| 8. Incorporate Changes into the Culture | Integrate into all communications. |

# Step 1: Create a Sense of Urgency

Organizational leaders need to make the case for change, create a sense of urgency and lay the foundation for employee participation going forward. This goal can be accomplished through a series of carefully crafted messages and well-coordinated internal communication. Employees should be made to feel a little uncomfortable with the status quo so they are more willing to let go of it. The messages should explain the forces causing the need for a change and begin to talk about the steps that will be taken to meet the challenge. Perhaps the organization already has set the stage and communicated some of these changes through industry news and business results. Specific examples of the forces causing the change that employees can relate to will help make the case.

The customer's voice can sometimes be used to make a case for change. Here are three examples, adapted from the author's personal experience, that vividly demonstrate how the customer can be used to communicate to employees:

- **Example #1:** At a managers' meeting, an airline shared letters from business travelers whose livelihoods were threatened and leisure passengers whose family vacations were ruined because of late flights to illustrate the need for an on-time performance initiative.

- **Example #2:** A utility company brought in a CEO of a microchip manufacturer to speak at a managers' meeting about how the company lost $1 million in productivity for every hour its plant was without power.

- **Example #3:** A large retail company hired a comedic actress to perform at a managers' meeting by playing the role of the company's target customer. The actress was able to deliver change messages from a customer's perspective in a pointed and sometimes outlandish manner that resonated with the employees. She could say things management couldn't.

Change messages from an organization's leaders should seek to be inclusive and connote an atmosphere of "We're all in this together." The messages should create a sense of urgency, but not panic, by explaining what happens if no action is taken. Employees should know what they stand to lose and what they may have to leave behind. Communications should convey a sense of hope and encourage an ongoing dialogue.

Figure 9.2 shows some key messages that make a case for change, create a sense of urgency, and lay the foundation for employee involvement going forward. Note the use of "our" and "we" to connote inclusiveness. The messages acknowledge the difficulty of change but have an optimistic tone at the same time. They talk about the next steps and encourage employee feedback and participation. You can use these key messages as the basis for creating customized key messages for your organization.

### Figure 9.2 Key Messages for Change

- The world around us is changing, and the demands on our business have never been greater. You've probably noticed the impacts these changes are already having on specific areas of our business.

- If we are to survive in the future, we cannot continue operating our business the same way. Even the very best of today will not be good enough for tomorrow. We must do better and we must start today.

- It takes time for major changes to take effect. We can see the iceberg ahead; we must start turning right now to avoid it.

- We must transform to meet the needs of our customers today and in the future. This transformation is critical to our continued success.

- We are on solid financial footing and we are well-positioned to make these changes. We can do this. And when we do, we will emerge from this transformation stronger than ever.

- We are striving to achieve results never before accomplished, so we will need to employ methods we have never before attempted. This may be uncomfortable at times, but it is also exciting.

- As with any major change, there will be ups and down along the way. And, as with anything new, there will be risks. But the biggest risk of all is doing nothing.

- Change is never easy, and it will take time to accomplish all we need to do. The length of time it takes to change can be frustrating at times. The key to success is our ability to rally together and stay the course until the work is done.

- We are forming a cross-functional team representing every major workgroup in the organization to devise a strategy and an action plan to take us where we need to be. Some of you may be asked to serve on that team. The team has the full support of senior leadership to do what needs to be done.

- You undoubtedly have a lot of questions about what this all means to you and what's going to happen next. We promise to keep an open dialogue with you going forward, and we encourage you to talk to your supervisor as well.

- Communication will be key to our transformation efforts. No one knows your job as well as you do, so we need your ideas to make this all work.

- This is an exciting time to be at this organization. Let's get to work!

Getting buy-in from employees is crucial if a sense of urgency is to be felt throughout the entire organization. If employees aren't convinced change needs to happen, it won't. Change, at least long-lasting and meaningful change, can't be mandated or coerced by management. Buy-in begins to happen when employees have had all their questions about the problem answered and when they feel they are being made part of the solution. Therefore, channels that accommodate questions and facilitate ongoing discussions should be used.

Face-to-face channels such as manager meetings and employee town hall sessions can be effective ways to begin the buy-in process because they are personal and allow for interactivity, including Q&A sessions and employee comments. A face-to-face meeting with a leader sends a message all by itself. It demonstrates to employees how important the message is, how much the leader cares about the change and that the leader respects the employees enough to talk directly with them. After all, if the employees weren't important, the leader wouldn't waste time speaking to them. In addition, a face-to-face meeting gives the leader an opportunity to obtain real time feedback. As the leader delivers key messages, he or she can see heads nodding, facial expressions changing and pick up on other non-verbal cues that tell how employees are responding to what they are hearing. Good leaders can adjust the messages' delivery on the fly based on the real time feedback they are receiving. Electronic channels, such as blogs and podcasts, can be effective follow-ups to face-to-face presentation because they allow for comments and ongoing discussions to occur.

> A face-to-face meeting with a leader sends a message all by itself. It demonstrates to employees how important the message is, how much the leader cares about the change and that the leader respects the employees enough to talk directly with them.

Figure 9.3 shows an example of a meeting discussion guide created for area superintendents of the fictitious ABC School District. Each of the area superintendents is to use the discussion guide to conduct a meeting with their principals to announce the launch of a major change initiative. The meeting's goal is to begin to get buy-in from the principals by informing and, more importantly, by involving them in the process. The guide is much more than a script. It contains ways to stimulate interactivity and try to get the principals to personalize the change and begin to own it. It also includes a PowerPoint presentation and a video.

## Figure 9.3 ABC School District Discussion Guide

### Meeting Discussion Guide

*This guide will help you as an area superintendent to facilitate discussions with your principal about our transformation project. It is designed to put information into context for your area and to drive conversations, deeper understanding and commitment. The italic text is for your reference and the plain text statements are messages for you to put into your own words. Please schedule your meeting to occur by the end of the month. To prepare for the meeting, you will need to download the PowerPoint and the video from the district intranet.*

### Welcome and Introduction

*Welcome everyone. Introduce any guests in attendance and any new principals. Recognize principals for any recent achievements made by their schools or teachers.*

We are about to begin a very exciting school year filled with great challenges and great opportunities. Today, I want to discuss where we are headed and get some feedback from you.

### The Imperative for Change

As you know, the world around us has changed dramatically with new technologies, global competition and new economic realities. The demands on education have never been greater. *At this point of the meeting, you may want to talk about changes you've seen in education during your career or you may want to ask a principal with a long-service record to reflect on changes he or she has seen. Make it personal.*

No one knows exactly what the future holds, but one thing is certain—like the rest of the world, we must continue to change. Our students are counting on us to prepare them for the world that will await them. Think about it: the students entering kindergarten right now will graduate in 2027. What kind of a world will be awaiting them? Will they be ready? Will we have done everything we can to prepare them adequately?

### Transformation

We are all part of an important mission to transform our schools to a system that meets students' needs today and for the future. Our graduates must be college and career ready. This transformation is critical to their futures and to our state's economic future.

As you know, a number of strategies are underway and some new ones will begin this year. Each individual initiative is part of a larger plan and they are all building upon one another. *You may want to mention some specific initiatives underway as examples.* It is important that everyone understand how all these pieces fit together, where we're going and how we're going to get there.

We're going to ask each of you to talk about our transformation efforts at your First Day of School Meeting with all your teachers. To help you, we've prepared a video with an address from the superintendent that explains our transformation project. Let's have a look at it.

*Play video message. At the conclusion, ask for comments on the message. Does this help put things in context?*

### What We Hope to Achieve

We are focusing on our students, our future and the promise we are making. Let's look at each of these areas:
- Our Students. All students can and must achieve college and career readiness. That is our goal.
- Our Future. College and career-ready graduates are the key to our state's long-term sustainability.
- Our Promise. We must work together, every step of the way—from K to 12—if we are to be successful.

**Putting It All Together**
How will we fulfill our promise? *Show next PowerPoint Slide.* Here are some of the ways.

One of these ways we introduced last year—the new principal evaluation plan.
At the leadership level, we are making sure our District Strategic Plan, our Area Plan and our school's Academic and Financial Plans are aligned and working together. *At this point of the meeting, you may want to discuss some of the high-level details of your Area Plan.*

As you know, we are making a major transformational shift. Student success won't be measured on arbitrary numbers, but will be measured on the students' ability to strive and reach higher. Our state and a handful of other states are on the leading edge of this change.

We cannot do this alone. We need GREAT teachers, GREAT leaders, and GREAT partnerships.


**Educator Effectiveness**
*Show next PowerPoint Slide.* The Educator Effectiveness package is a great example of how we're meeting the needs of today but also building for the future.
1. Student Growth Percentile (SGP)
2. Charlotte Danielson Observation Protocol
3. Tripod Student Surveys
4. Student Learning Outcomes (SLO)


**Feedback and Discussion**
Now I want to hear from you. *Ask the following questions and facilitate discussion.* What questions do you have? What are your personal reflections?

We're going to break into small groups for just a few minutes. I'd like the elementary principals to meet over there, the middle school principals over there and the high school principals to meet over there. I want you to discuss your thoughts on how these goals are specific to your school levels and how you can implement them. Then we'll regroup to wrap things up. *Monitor the discussions, and when they seem to be concluding, call the group back together.*


**Next Steps**
*Regroup the participants.* As I mentioned before, we're asking each of you to communicate the direction we're going to your teachers. It is important that everyone understands we have a goal and a plan to get there. But it will take all of us, working together, to succeed.

So, to help you communicate all of this to your teachers, we've prepared a discussion guide for you to follow that is supported with the video we saw earlier and a PowerPoint. As you conduct these meetings, we want you to write down some of the feedback you receive. We don't need names. We're just looking for overall reactions. Are our messages being understood? Is there confusion about any of this? We want you to capture that feedback and send it to me. I also want you to ask your teachers how they personally plan to strive higher. I'll then present all of this at our leadership meeting and we'll compare it to feedback from the other schools.

In addition to communication, we need to ensure that these principles are put in place at every school. These are the grounding principles that will guide all of our transformation and improvement efforts. Each of you is tasked to develop an improvement plan that includes every one of these critical elements in order for us to succeed. We are continuing to build on our foundation. We are building a bridge to the future.

So, we've got a very exciting year ahead of us and I'm looking forward to working with each and every one of you. Thank you!

## Step 2: Create a Guiding Coalition

The second step in Kotter's model is creating a guiding coalition, a group with enough power to enact the change that is sought. Organizations often form these groups as a cross-functional task team, and sometimes a member of the executive team with a vested interest in the change is appointed as the team's champion. Ideally, an internal communication professional should be part of the task team or, at the very least, made available to the task team as a valuable resource.

Kotter says four qualities must be in place for the team to be effective:

1. Position Power: Enough key players should be on board so those left out cannot block progress.

2. Expertise: All relevant points of view should be represented so informed intelligent decisions can be made.

3. Credibility: The group should be seen and respected by those in the firm so other employees will take the group's pronouncements seriously.

4. Leadership: The group should have enough proven leaders to be able to drive the change process.

In a large organization, not every employee will know the employees who have been selected to serve on the task team and their credentials, particularly those employees who are not from their workgroup. The internal communication professionals can help the task team achieve recognition and credibility with the rest of the organization through appropriate communications. For instance, they could include photos of each team member on the organization's intranet listing the workgroups each member represents and detailing each member's areas of expertise. For even more depth, they could record a podcast that includes an interview with each team member talking about his or her experience with the organization and what he or she hopes to accomplish as part of the task team.

## Step 3: Develop a Change Vision

The first action item for the cross-functional task team is to develop a change vision. Kotter says the vision should fulfill three purposes:

1. Simplify hundreds or maybe thousands of detailed discussions.

2. Motivate employees to take action even if the initial steps are painful.

3. Coordinate the actions of different people in a remarkably fast and efficient way.

Internal communication professionals are in a perfect position to help draft the precise language of the vision statement and ensure it is easy to explain, easy to understand and inspirational enough to generate employee engagement. Internal communication professionals also are in a position to coordinate other communication resources as well, including graphic artists who may be able to find creative ways to express the vision visually.

Logos and slogans are often misused and overused by amateurs, but talented communicators and graphic artists can use them to create powerful ways to communicate a vision that is meaningful and motivational to employees. Figure 9.4 shows an example of an effective use of a slogan and a logo.

**Figure 9.4: Effective Use of Logo and Slogan**

**ZERO AND BEYOND**

The Zero and Beyond logo is a powerful visual reminder of our goal. We realize that it will take much more than a logo to achieve our goal. However, a logo can be a powerful communication vehicle, if used consistently. As we become used to seeing a particular symbol or logo, it gains more power and meaning.

The dramatic heart motif vividly expresses the key principles of Zero and Beyond. With just one continuous stroke, the symbol, at first, seems quite simple. But the longer you look, the more you see. The Zero and Beyond symbol depicts these themes:

The heart is a life-giving and life-sustaining organ. Its shape is a universal symbol of caring. The bold outline signifies strength, but keeps the logo gender-neutral.

The zero literally communicates zero – zero fatalities, zero injuries, zero incidents and zero job-related illnesses at work and at home.

The logo was interesting in several ways. Its modern look was atypical for the company and instantly told employees this initiative was different. But more notable were the optical illusions contained in the logo. Employees quickly noted the negative space in the logo resembled a person making a zero sign over his head as if to say, "That is our goal." Others said the negative space depicted a person from behind who was reaching out to embrace others as if to say, "We need to care for one another," which was one of the initiative's key messages.

Employees were excited about the logo and they became eager to explain its meaning to others. The logo served as a constant reminder to work safely and to care for one another. The logo became so popular that it was duplicated on hardhat stickers, bumper stickers, safety goggles, coffee mugs and even company water towers at various mining sites.

The company dramatically improved safety awareness and its safety record. Safety became a part of the company's culture. The company became a model to follow in the mining and manufacturing industries.

## Step 4: Communicate the Vision

While Kotter's eight steps are a guide to the overall process of achieving effective change for the organization, they don't delve into the specific stages the employees themselves must go through to reach engagement and embrace change. For that, you need a change communication process such as the one developed by Thomas J. Lee (Arceil Leadership Ltd., 2010) to augment Kotter's Step 4. Lee's process has helped me guide my thinking and allowed me to create powerful strategies.

Lee's process reveals that employees must move through the following four stages before they reach engagement and embrace change: awareness (in our eyes), understanding (in our minds), acceptance (in our hearts) and commitment (in our work). Employees move through these steps sequentially and each stage takes time to achieve. You cannot skip a step. If you want employees to be committed to a particular change, they must first be aware of it, then understand it and then accept it.

Organizations can move employees through the four stages with effective communication. It must be understood that communication is defined as anything that conveys meaning, and organizations do plenty of things that convey meaning. Lee breaks down organizational communication in three parts: formal, semi-formal and informal. It's important to understand all three when formulating change communication plans.

Formal communication includes the things internal communicators oversee such as newsletters, intranets, podcasts and town hall meetings. Formal communication also includes things internal communicators don't oversee including brand promises, business plans, and awards and recognition programs. Formal communication is important to make everyone aware of a change effort, and it can be effective at driving deeper understanding. But the success of formal communication begins to wane in the acceptance stage and has little or no affect in the commitment stage. To reach the latter stages, an organization needs to have effective semi-formal and informal communication.

Semi-formal communication includes the pay scale, employee benefits offerings, policies and procedures, the decision-making process and quality standards. Alignment occurs when an organization's "do" matches its "say." If aligned with the formal communication, semi-formal communication can move employees to complete understanding and acceptance and begin to instill commitment. If not aligned, it can undermine the formal communication and derail a change effort quickly. Employees realize a change effort is just "lip service" when the semi-formal communication is not aligned with the formal communication. A lot of employee angst in an organization can be traced to a misalignment of the formal and semi-formal communication.

Informal communication is a little trickier. It includes visible behaviors and values, inclusion and collaboration, resources and support, risk tolerance, transparency and authenticity. When informal, semi-formal and formal communication is aligned, employees can be moved to the commitment stage. Commitment is possible when what's going on in the halls aligns with the mission statement and values posted on the walls. And, of course, misaligned informal communication can undermine everything.

Understanding this process helps us to identify unintended, and previously unnoticed, credibility gaps including mixed, muddled and mute messages that your organization may be sending. This understanding allows you to be a better executive counselor to your leadership team. It also helps you to set appropriate expectations for what can and cannot be achieved with formal communication alone. For instance, if a change effort is launched to bolster customer service, but the organization fails to fund the necessary changes or empower employees accordingly, then the effort likely will fail no matter how good your formal communication efforts are.

The process also shows us once again that we need to win heads and hearts to move employees to change. The famous Canadian neurologist Donald B. Calne said reason leads people to conclusions, but emotion leads them to action. Or, as Kotter puts it, "People change what they do less because they are given analysis that shifts their thinking than because they are shown a truth that influences their feelings." An organization's formal communication is effective for making the logical case for change, but it will take emotion, driven by semi-formal and informal communication in the organization, to move employees to action.

When formal, semi-formal and informal communication is working together in an integrated fashion, the stage is set for engagement. Lee says alignment of formal, semi-formal and informal communication is needed for an organization to stay in business for the long term. Engagement is needed for growth. Once alignment is achieved, leadership drives engagement. With the help of their internal communicators, leaders create a clear vision of where they want to go, communicate that vision logically and emotionally, and ensure that organizational behaviors are consistent as employees work to change behaviors and achieve the vision.

**The Change Communication Plan:** With an understanding of Lee's process, you can take the strategic internal communication planning process detailed in Chapter 5 and begin to determine the most effective ways to communicate a change vision in your organization.

Let's look at the steps in the strategic internal communication plan template again and see how the idea of change communication might be applied to them:

- **Title:** The change vision might be the title.

- **Project Team:** The cross-functional task team likely will be the team crafting the communication plan.

- **Situational Analysis:** The detailed analysis should include the reasons driving the change. The internal communication professional also may want to conduct a focus group to establish a baseline of employee perceptions.

- **Objectives:** This section may help to flush out the change vision.
- **Goals:** The desired outcomes of the communication plan should be specific to the change process.
- **Target Audience Analysis:** The audience analysis should pay particular attention to groups primarily affected by the change and secondary groups. Also of note are audiences that may emerge as resisters to the change, such as unions.
- **Key Messages:** The generic key messages regarding change in Figure 9.2 should be helping in developing the key messages.
- **Strategies and Tactics:** Will be specific to driving change.
- **Action Planning and Timeline:** The timeline includes ways to keep the change effort "evergreen" in the months following the launch of the change initiative.
- **Budget:** The funding for the initiative should reflect that change efforts take time.
- **Evaluation Plan:** The evaluation should include a way to measure employee perceptions about the change before and after the initiative is launched.
- **Project Approval Checklist:** The approval checklist should include the cross-functional task team members.

## Formulating Strategies and Tactics

Following are some tips specific to change communication to keep in mind when formulating the strategies and tactics section of the strategic communication plan:

- Focus on communication that involves, not just informs, employees. Strive for communication that includes employees in activities such as focus groups, surveys, Q&As and ongoing discussions. Use internal social media platforms, hotlines, etc.
- Personalize change whenever possible. Show the relevancy to individual jobs.

- Use vivid storytelling techniques to paint a picture of the vision. Stories can be more powerful than data. Metaphors, analogies and examples all help employees to see the desired state in their mind's eye. Employees are more apt to take the journey if they know where they are going.

- Look for living examples and other ways to model the attitudes and behaviors the organization is trying to create. Be specific about what you want employees to do. Create a list of behaviors to stop doing, start doing and continue doing.

- It is more important to change hearts than it is to change minds. Storytelling, posters, dramatic videos and other communication techniques that evoke an emotional response can be effective. Kotter says the most effective mix is a 60% focus on changing hearts and a 40% focus on changing minds.

- Identify aspects of the change that already dwell in the employees' hearts. It's easier to resonate than it is to persuade.

- Listen to what employees are saying about the change.

- Cut the clutter from communication channels so competing voices don't drown out important change messages.

- Minimize uncertainty as much as possible. Weiss says it is ambiguity, not change, that causes employees to resist.

- Respect the intellect of employees. Address areas of anxiety, anger and mistrust.

- Be respectful of the past. A transformation is needed because the situation has changed. The old ways of doing things probably were the right ways to do things in their time.

- Celebrate successes along the way to model behavior and to keep momentum going.

- Recognize the Cultural Warriors who are embracing the change. Motivate them to help make the change happen. Look for other influential employees and enlist them as Cultural Warriors as well.

- Look for "evergreen" communications such as progress charts, checklist updates, etc. Centralize information in microsites.

# Step 5: Empower Broad-Based Power

The task team must be empowered to do what is necessary to help enact the change. It must remove barriers, including structural barriers and troublesome supervisors who may be blocking progress.

You can help in this stage by continuing to communicate the progress made by the task team and continuing to look for ways to establish their credibility. In addition, the employee communicators should make sure that communication policies and systems aren't acting as barriers to the change effort.

The Arceil Rainbow model will again be helpful in understanding how an organization's "do" must match its "say." Communicators can work with their organizational development partners to point out barriers undermining the credibility of the change messages. A message without credibility is meaningless no matter how elegantly stated.

# Step 6: Generate Short-Term Wins

Step 6 in Kotter's approach is to generate some short-term wins to keep the momentum of the change effort going. Kotter says that change efforts have a much better chance to succeed in the long term if short-term wins are achieved. But those short-term wins will be meaningless if others in the organization don't know about them.

Internal communication professionals must communicate the short-term successes and ensure they are clearly tied back to the vision. The strategic internal communication plan devised in Step 4 should have included ways to communicate the short-term successes.

Special care should be taken to make sure the communications are permeating to all levels of the organization in memorable and lasting ways. Kotter says it is common for leaders to believe they have communicated adequately, but in reality, employees who are three levels below the CEO may have never heard of the changes. Thomas Lee of Arceil Communications agrees. "It is a matter of repetition, reiteration, and redundancy. Saying it once is tantamount to never saying it at all. You must say it over and over and over. When you think you have it said too many times, you're just getting started."

All too often, short-term successes are communicated to employees, but several weeks later, they forget about them. Then they complain that the company made a big deal out of its change plan, but nothing ever came of it. It likely will take repeated communication efforts in visible places to make sure success stories are being heard throughout the organization. Placing a large progress chart on an easel by a security gate, through which every employee has to pass to gain entry to the facility, and updating the chart daily, showing the achievements made in the change initiative, is a good example of a repeated communication effort in a highly visible place.

## Step 7: Never Let Up

Step 7 is to consolidate gains and produce more and more change. Leaders need to continue to create projects and drive change efforts deeper into the organization. Once again, the successful implementation of additional change will need to be communicated to the organization.

The strategic internal communication plan devised in Step 4 should have included ways to keep the change effort in front of employees on an ongoing basis. For example, Phelps Dodge once instituted a rule that every company meeting must begin with a "safety share." Employees of the copper mining company took turns sharing brief safety tips for the workplace and for the home. This activity not only allowed employees to learn new safety behaviors, but it also reinforced the safety initiative repeatedly until the initiative became part of the company's culture.

## Step 8: Incorporate Changes into the Culture

Long-term success will occur only after a majority of an organization's members truly embrace the change and begin to live the vision in their day-to-day lives. The internal communication role in this final step is to ensure that the change vision is integrated and embedded in every internal communication produced. The internal communication professionals also should look at ways to reward and recognize employees who are "living the vision."

However, as pointed out in the Arceil Rainbow, the most effective communication at this stage is the informal voice of the organization.

# Chapter Conclusion

Change is a never-ending process and never comfortable, so organizations must constantly adapt and learn to be comfortable with being uncomfortable. Change can be a highly emotional experience for individuals and organizations. We can tap into that emotion to help affect change. As the famous French writer Anatole France once said, "To accomplish great things, we must not only act but also dream; not only plan but also believe."

Having expertise in change communication is crucial to maximizing internal communication. Understanding Kotter's eight-step model, the Arceil Rainbow and the change tips presented in this chapter will help you create powerful communication strategies to propel change in your organization. You can easily adapt the change talking points and the sample change discussion guide presented in this chapter for your organization.

Most change efforts fail to reach expectations. You can greatly increase the odds of success by ensuring that change projects are communicated effectively.

## Chapter Exercises

XYZ Corp. is changing the way it pays its hourly employees. XYZ has been issuing paper paychecks to employees since the company began operations 20 years ago. For the past five years, employees have had the option of choosing to have their paychecks issued as an electronic direct deposit to their checking accounts. Only about 10% of employees have elected that option. The company wants to end the paper checks entirely and switch to an electronic direct deposit system for all employees. XYZ business analysts estimate the switch will save the company nearly $2 million a year in printing and mailing costs. The company has been losing money the past six quarters. This switch would help the company to return to profitability.

- Use the generic key messages in Figure 9.2 to write five key messages for this change effort.

_____

_____

_____

_____

_____

- List some ways employees could be involved in this change process.

_____

_____

_____

_____

## Chapter References

Arceil Leadership Ltd., "The Three Voices of Every Company" retrieved July 1, 2013, from http://rainbows.typepad.com/blog/2010/03/the-three-voices-of-every-company.html

Cohen, D. S., & Kotter, J. P. (2002). *The Heart of Change: Real-Life Stories of How People Change Their Organizations*. Harvard Business School Press Books, 1.

D'Aprix, R. (1996). *Communicating for Change: Connecting the workplace with the marketplace*. New York: Jossey-Bass Management.

Weiss, A. (2002). *Process Consulting*. San Francisco: Jossey-Bass/Pfeiffer.

## Chapter 10

# Evaluating Internal Communication Effectiveness

"When you take the time to actually listen,
with humility, to what people have to say,
it's amazing what you can learn."
– Greg Mortenson

**Chapter Overview:** If you are trying to maximize your internal communication efforts, you must know how to evaluate your work so it can be improved upon, adapted and replicated. In addition, you must demonstrate the effectiveness of your communication efforts to your internal clients and to your senior leadership team if you want to gain credibility, trust, respect and autonomy.

In this chapter, you'll learn the importance of evaluating internal communication strategies, why you should measure, what you should measure, when you should measure, who should conduct the evaluations, what types of data you should collect, common measurement methods, and how to measure employee engagement.

The only way internal communication professionals and those who pay for their services can know whether their communication strategies are successful is by evaluating message effectiveness, business impact, and changes in awareness, depth of understanding, perceptions, attitudes, beliefs, workplace behaviors, commitment and the level of employee engagement.

When you are trying to maximize internal communication, you must focus on outcomes, not outputs. In other words, you should not be nearly as concerned with how many times an article appeared in the company newsletter or how many times the home page of the intranet was visited as you are about the impact your communication strategies are having on workplace behaviors, such as activities that affect productivity, employee participation, customer service, safety, absenteeism, employee theft, task compliance or employee retention.

Of course, how many times a message is communicated (frequency) and how many employees receive a message (saturation) are important for the initial awareness stage because if a message isn't received, it can't be acted upon. But message frequency and saturation are only the means to greater ends.

Many factors affect employee engagement, but communication is the overriding factor. For instance, the organization's strategic direction and a belief in its leadership are critical factors in engagement, but without effective communication, employees won't understand what the strategic direction is or have faith in their leadership. Also, for this book's purposes, communication is being broadly defined. Everything an organization does is communicating something to employees. An organization's working conditions, employee benefits offerings, policies and procedures, taboo topics and unwritten rules are all forms of communicating. Employees know whether an organization's actions are aligned with its value claims. What attributes get an employee hired, the accomplishments that get an employee promoted and the specific actions that can get an employee fired speak volumes about what an organization really stands for.

Figure 10.1 shows the steps employees must go through to reach engagement. Awareness is a necessary precursor to a greater depth of understanding; understanding is necessary to change perceptions, attitudes and beliefs; perceptions, attitudes and beliefs must be changed for workplace behavior to change; and appropriate workplace behaviors lead to organizational commitment. When all of these stages are fulfilled, an organization can reach employee engagement. An employee communicator could measure any one of the stages, and a positive result would indicate that the preceding steps had been fulfilled. For instance, if research reveals a deep understanding of a subject, the researchers can safely assume that awareness also has been fulfilled. After all, employees can't have a deep level of understanding of something of which they aren't aware.

**Figure 10.1: Steps to Engagement**

| TYPES OF MEASURES | REQUIRED POSITIVE RESULTS |
|---|---|
| Awareness | Awareness |
| Depth of Understanding | Awareness, depth of understanding |
| Perceptions | Awareness, depth of understanding, perceptions |
| Attitudes | Awareness, depth of understanding, perceptions, attitudes |
| Beliefs | Awareness, depth of understanding, perceptions, attitudes, beliefs |
| Workplace Behaviors | Awareness, depth of understanding, perceptions, attitudes, beliefs, workplace behaviors |
| Commitment | Awareness, depth of understanding, perceptions, attitudes, beliefs, workplace behaviors, commitment |
| Employee Engagement | Awareness, depth of understanding, perceptions, attitudes, beliefs, workplace behaviors, commitment, employee engagement |

# Understanding Why We Measure

Communicators gather feedback and measure the effectiveness of their efforts to make improvements to communication processes and messages. They replicate their successes and prove their worth to their organizations to help them maintain credibility and gain further support.

As shown in the strategic communication model in Chapter 5 (Figure 5.1), evaluation is part of a continuous cycle of communicating, measuring and refreshing messages. Therefore, the act of measuring and the continuous improvement that follows can contribute to more effective communication. If all communication goals and business objectives are achieved, then the process can be documented and applied to similar projects.

Return on Investment: As an internal communication professional, you may be asked to quantify the value of your communication efforts to demonstrate a return on investment (ROI), particularly for large capital expenses such as an enterprise-wide intranet. ROI is the way executives tend to think about projects and budgets, including communication projects. While employee communicators don't directly generate revenue, their efforts can improve workplace productivity and participation in work-related activities, reduce turnover and absenteeism, and enhance customer service and brand reputation. Estimated dollar amounts can be affixed to these outcomes. In addition, there are costs associated with not communicating. For instance, a failure to communicate could cause employees to be confused about what to do, resulting in inefficiencies and errors. Estimated dollar amounts can be affixed to those negative aspects as well. If the benefits of communicating outweigh the costs of communicating, then there is positive ROI.

**Measuring the Value of Communication:** Many employee communicators are reluctant to measure ROI because it doesn't include the relative worth of their communications. Communication consultant Lorenzo Sierra, ABC, put it this way: "Organizational communication is a lot like love. You really can't quantify it with raw numbers, but you need it to survive" (Sierra, 2003). Sierra devised his own formula to calculate the value of communication: $V=(c + e)p$. In the equation, $V$ (the value communication) equals the costs plus the efforts of what you're communicating to the power of perception.

The value of communication is the monetary and anecdotal worth of what you're communicating. The cost includes the worth of what's being communicated. For instance, if an organization is communicating about a health plan and the health plan costs $1 million annually, then that is the cost. The danger in not communicating about the health plan is that employees may not know how to use it properly; therefore, it is no longer the competitor differentiator it was meant to be. That would mean the $1 million was squandered. The effort in communicating includes the monetary costs (employee salary, benefits, etc.), and anecdotal costs related to organizational well-being. The perception element refers to the gap between expectations and reality. The employee communicator's job is to narrow that gap as much as possible.

# Determining What to Measure
Communicators who wish to measure effectiveness focus on three areas:

- **Message Effectiveness:**
    - Were all the necessary audiences being reached?
    - Were the messages conducive to the organizational culture and climate? Was the timing of the messages right? Were other activities

occurring in the organization that diluted or distorted the messages or distracted attention from them?
- Were the right communication channels used? Did they reach the intended audiences? Were the channels appropriate for the message they carried? Was the infrastructure for the channels functioning properly? Were there adequate staff resources and a budget to support the channels?
- Were the messages perceived as intended or do they need to be refreshed or recast? Were the messages clear? Were there cultural aspects that caused the messages to be misunderstood? Did the messages cause additional questions to be asked that need to be addressed?

- **Business Impact:** The impact on specific business measures such as productivity, cost reduction, sales, customer-service scores, brand reputation, quality assurance, lost-time injuries, safety audits, absenteeism, employee theft, task compliance and employee retention. The employee communicators don't create new ways to measure business impact, but they do tap into the organization's existing method for collecting such data.

- **Communication Goals:** Specific goals including changes in awareness, depth of understanding, perceptions, attitudes, beliefs, workplace behaviors, commitment or level of engagement.

## Deciding Who Measures

You need to devise various approaches to collect and analyze data on an ongoing basis as part of your job. In many cases, you will be able to handle the evaluation and measurement yourself. In other cases, you will want to partner with human resources or other functional areas in your organization that may be collecting similar data. For instance, human resources groups often conduct annual "People Pulse" or "Temperature" surveys designed to measure employee morale, commitment and engagement. By partnering with them, you may be able to tack on some survey questions related to internal communication or you might be able to suggest subtle wording changes that will help yield more valuable data.

Measurement is increasingly becoming part of the job description for employee communicators, but communicators aren't statisticians. You likely do not have the tools, knowledge or capacity to handle large-scale measurement projects involving focus groups at multiple locations, organization-wide surveys and complex data analysis. You likely will want to enlist the help of a professional consulting firm for large-scale measurement projects. Outside vendors can be costly, but they can provide many advantages that may yield more accurate and more useful data.

Here are some of the advantages of using a professional firm:

- **Impartial and Confidential:** Employees may be more willing to provide honest and candid information to a third-party vendor who is perceived to be impartial and who will keep the names of individual participants confidential. Many professional firms participate in a certification program called Safe Harbor that further ensures employee confidentiality (Robert Berrier, Spring International, personal conversation, March 11, 2014).

- **Expertise and Capability:** Professional measurement vendors will possess expertise in research techniques, focus group facilitation, survey design and question writing, statistically valid data collection and statistical analysis. They will have the systems in place to collect data online, by phone or hardcopy, and they will have sophisticated software to analyze the data.

- **Comparative Data:** Large measurement firms will be able to compare data from one organization to data from other organizations of similar size, in the same geographical area or in the same industry.

## Committing to Measuring

A common mistake among employee communicators is to get so caught up in their busy schedules that they miss opportunities to measure and obtain solid data on their communication messages. According to measurement expert Angela Sinickas, the No. 1 measurement mistake communicators make is forgetting to obtain baseline measurements before beginning a major communication campaign (Sinickas, 2010).

Figure 10.2 shows when and why you should consider collecting measurement data.

**Figure 10.2: When and Why to Collect Measurement Data**

| WHEN | WHY |
|---|---|
| Before beginning a major communication campaign. | To obtain information that may help formulate communication strategy and to collect data to establish a baseline for later comparison. |
| At intervals of a major communication campaign: effectiveness and whether adjustments need to be made. | To track progress toward communication goals and business objectives and to determine message. |
| At the conclusion of a major communication campaign. | To determine whether communication goals and business objectives were met and to determine message effectiveness. |
| At the conclusion of employee communication events such as all-manager meetings, employee town halls, all-hands meetings and organization-wide webcasts. | To determine employee participation and message effectiveness. |
| After the conclusion of significant business events such as crises, organizational restructurings, staff layoffs, mergers or acquisitions. | To determine employee perceptions, attitudes, beliefs, level of commitment or engagement. |
| At daily, weekly, monthly, quarterly and annual intervals: | To analyze digital data and uncover trends that can be helpful in formulating communication strategies. |
| Annually at the conclusion of natural business cycles. | To determine the organization's pulse so new communication strategies can be formulated for the next cycle. |
| Whenever anecdotal feedback presents itself. | So it can be analyzed periodically to uncover trends, perceptions and opportunities to improve processes. |

# Understanding What to Collect: Quantitative and Qualitative Data

The type of data collected can be categorized as either quantitative or qualitative. Quantitative deals with data that can be measured and expressed as figures. Qualitative deals with data that can be observed and expressed as descriptions, perceptions or feelings. For instance, quantitative data would reveal the exact number of employees who listened to a monthly CEO webcast, but qualitative data would include what they remember most about the webcast.

Figure 10.3 shows an example of an evaluation of a monthly webcast/conference call that was held by the fictitious ABC Airline. Employees can view the webcast over the internet, or they can call in and listen via telephone. The ABC Airline employee communicators designed this brief analysis to be sent by e-mail to the company's busy executive team. It begins with a short subjective analysis of the event. The table includes quantitative data and is designed to be expanded with each new webcast/conference call so participation trends can be revealed over time. Qualitative data has been summarized at the end.

## Figure 10.3: Data Summary Example

### Monthly Webcast/Conference Call Participation Report and Feedback

**Analysis:** Participation was down by 100, probably due to the timing of the meeting—Monday morning, end of holiday weekend, conflicted with other meetings.

Participation among field stations was good. Feedback was positive and technical issues were isolated. More and more people are saying how much they prefer listening at their desks so they can work while they listen (like a podcast). Some departments are listening together in conference rooms, which is why there are more phone participants than phone lines. We are continuing to work with IT to upgrade speakers on the older computers in the maintenance facilities.

**Message Effectiveness:** Judging from the Q&A portion of the call and the anecdotal feedback we received, the key messages of the webcast were well-received. In particular, the slides on on-time performance, the ROI of the winglets and the Asian route expansion appear to have enhanced understanding.

| DATE | TOPICS | # PHONE LINES | # PHONE PARTICIPANTS | WEB PARTICIPANTS | LIVE-IN ROOM PARTICIPANTS | TOTAL |
|---|---|---|---|---|---|---|
| 8/18 | Q2 Financial Results | 53 | 95 | 80 | 14 | 189 |
| 7/24 | Jet Fuel Costs | 71 | 162 | 123 | 9 | 294 |
| 6/16 | On-Time Initiative | 84 | 227 | 115 | 8 | 350 |
| 5/15 | Route Expansion | 66 | 155 | 118 | 12 | 285 |

**Anecdotal Feedback:** We sent out an e-mail request following the webcast/conference call soliciting employee feedback and we received 23 replies. Following is a summary of those comments:

**Overall**
- Excellent opportunity to hear about important company actions/concerns.
- While much of the information is available in the news media, it is still valuable to see it related to us.
- If anything was missing from this one, it would be more about future plans.
- Like that you can listen while you work. Would rather work at my desk and listen than attend a live meeting. More productivity that way.
- Great form of communication for us at field stations.
- The worst thing a company can do for employee morale is keep secrets and ignore employee input. ABC does a good job to keep the flow of information open and still maintain a competitive edge.
- Always tune in to see where we stand financially; what are the plans to move forward and what specific areas in operations do we need to improve.
- Please keep the webcast. I listen to the replay at a convenient time. Very informative.
- Really appreciate hearing the CEO himself talk about these items.
- This is a great way to increase our understanding of what goes on in other departments and why we are doing what we're doing.
- This is a very good means of communicating between upper management and us.
- This is a great way to communicate without having to bring everyone together in one place.

**What Stood Out on the Call?**
- The big message that stood out was that we've slipped in our on-time performance over the last month and need to make some improvements. (Reported by 21 of the respondents.)
- It is great to get to hear explanations of why we placed an order for additional winglets. I had no idea of the fuel savings prior to the webcast. Really liked the slide that showed the savings per flight.
- I understand now why we are trying to expand with new Asian routes.

**Q&A Portion**
- Today's questions were particularly good (hedging arrangements, chance/benefit of obtaining a/c earlier).
- The Q&A is my favorite.
- I thought the Q&A is a nice way to have direct communication with Senior Management.

**Technology**
- Everything worked properly. It was very easy to log on.
- Don't have speakers on my computer so we listened on the phone and watched on the computer.
- The sound quality on the webcast is not so great since we depend on the built-in speakers on our desktops.

**Why didn't you participate?**
- Did not participate due to an FAA audit that was requested only this morning. Will look at the archive presentation of the webcast.
- Operations departments were on the daily Ops Call. That included about 40 people who typically participate in the webcast.
- First thing Monday morning is not the best time for this meeting.
- The timing of the call interfered with the usual morning maintenance scheduling call.
- I just forgot about it. I will listen to the replay on the intranet.

**Questions?** You may ask questions or provide comments by replying to this e-mail. Please let us know if you'd like to see the complete spreadsheet list of participants. Thank you!

Employee communicators often think of quantitative data as information that determines what and qualitative data as information that determines why. Both the quantitative what and the qualitative why are needed to evaluate the effectiveness of communication strategies. Collecting the two types of data is often cyclical. For instance, qualitative data from an exploratory focus group may reveal some of the questions that need to be asked on a follow-up survey and the quantitative results from that survey may require further explanation that can best be derived from additional focus groups. The whole process may repeat itself on an annual basis to determine progress.

# Determining Which Evaluation Tools to Use

You can use a number of methods to capture quantitative and qualitative data that can be used to formulate effective internal communication strategies.

Here are some common measurement methods:

- Anecdotal Feedback
- Focus Groups
- Online Polls
- Digital Analytics
- Surveys
- Communication Audits

Each of these measurement methods is useful for collecting particular types of data, and each has inherent strengths and weaknesses. Figure 10.4 shows a comparison of each of these collection methods.

## Figure 10.4: Evaluation Tools Comparison

| TOOLS | ANECDOTAL FEEDBACK | FOCUS GROUPS | ONLINE POLLS | DIGITAL ANALYTICS | SURVEYS | COMM AUDITS |
|---|---|---|---|---|---|---|
| **Type of Data Collected** | Qualitative | Qualitative | Quantitative | Qualitative and Quantitative | Qualitative and Quantitative | Qualitative and Quantitative |
| **Methods Conducted** | Feedback requests, unsolicited comments, observations, personal interviews | Informal or formal facilitated discussions | E-mail, online | Tracking software | Paper or online | Surveys, focus groups, observation, interviews analysis |
| **Primary Strengths** | Inexpensive and easy to gather, may point out other needed research | Illuminates issues, adds color to quantitative data, uncovers issues | Inexpensive, easy and fast way to get a snapshot of employee attitudes and interests | Built in to most systems, multitude of data | Versatile way to collect wide range of information | Highly accurate, complete picture |
| **Weaknesses** | Not statistically valid | Group dynamics affect data quality | Doesn't provide context, self-selected participants | Requires analysis and context | Can be expensive, time-consuming | Expensive, time-consuming |

Let's look at each measuring method and discuss how you can use it to enhance the effectiveness of your communication efforts.

Collecting Anecdotal Feedback: Anecdotal feedback is an inexpensive and easy way to gather qualitative information, and it is probably the most common way for you to get a feel for how your messages are being received, if your channels are functioning properly, if there are any credibility gaps between employees and leaders, and if the internal communication function is perceived as providing value to the organization.

Here are some common ways you can collect anecdotal feedback:

- **Observation and Listening:** Make it a practice to listen to employees whenever they are in the employee cafeteria, a break room, an employee shuttle bus, the hallways and anywhere else employees congregate and talk about workplace issues. Look for how communication is taking place within a workgroup—how do employees get information, are there team meetings, does the department produce its own newsletter or have its own intranet site, and so on. Check to see whether internal communication channels are working as intended. For example, are the company newsletters being delivered to employee workstations or are they being left in a pile somewhere? Do employees have the necessary hardware and software to access the CEO webcasts? Do employees really pay attention to the digital signage in the break room, or are they watching TV shows instead?

- **Spot Checking:** You can call employees at random after major announcements to see what they think or you can solicit feedback from employees via e-mail. You can develop a list of trusted employees to reach out to for perspective on issues in the organization. Find out what the latest rumors are. Take note of unsolicited comments you hear in meetings or receive via e-mail. Walk around the organization and talk to employees and observe them in their work environments.

- **Interviewing:** You can conduct periodic interviews with key internal clients and executive team members. Doing the interviews one-on-one will help ensure confidentiality. A good time to conduct such interviews is at the conclusion of a business cycle as the interviewee is preparing for the next cycle to begin. Ask questions about upcoming initiatives and major priorities, and how you can help.

By keeping a running log of all the anecdotal feedback you collect, you can look for patterns and trends. The log can be as simple as a word-processing document or a simple spreadsheet. You can simply copy and paste e-mail and blog comments into the log or type in a summary of comments you overhear.

Although anecdotal feedback is not a statistically valid way to gather research, it can help you to gain perspective and context, which in turn helps you to devise more effective communication strategies and craft more impactful messages.

**Conducting Focus Groups:** Focus group meetings can be an effective way to gather qualitative data that may illuminate organizational issues, provide color and context to previously gathered quantitative data or uncover a need for further research in specific areas. They can be informal pizza lunches with a small group of employees representing a cross-section of the organization, or they can be more formal and include a randomly selected sampling from the employee population. Large-scale measurement efforts might include focus group meetings held at every major workgroup or at every major work location or some combination thereof. When focus groups are done properly, they can provide good information. If the same finding comes out of several focus groups, this enhances the information's reliability.

Successful focus groups require a randomly selected group of participants (usually 6-12 employees), a skilled facilitator who will ensure all participants are heard and that the discussion is on topic, and a discussion guide designed to meet the objectives of the measurement effort. A word of caution: the artificial setting and group dynamics of a focus group can greatly affect the discussion, particularly with sensitive subjects, so the data are not always an accurate reflection of the attitudes, beliefs or perceptions of the entire organization. Often, follow-up research is required. It is common for issues raised by focus groups to become the basis for questions on follow-up surveys.

Another concern is that while focus groups allow the participants to feel that their opinions have been heard, others in the organization may feel left out. In many cases, the employee communicators will want to let the entire organization know that focus groups are being held and that they include a cross-section of the employee population. They also may want to post a summary of the comments obtained during the focus groups when they are concluded so everyone knows what issues were raised.

Focus groups involving managers or directors should be kept small, usually three to five participants. This size is recommended because managers and directors have a lot to offer and each likely will want to weigh in on most of the topics. It can be too time-consuming and frustrating for the participants if the group is too large.

**Posting Online Polls:** E-mail and online polls can be an inexpensive and fast method to obtain a lot of quantitative data, get a snapshot of organizational attitudes, provide some employee interactivity and add interest to an organization's intranet. A daily poll can be a readership builder for e-letters, online publications and intranet sites.

Many intranet platforms include built-in polling capabilities, and free online applications, such as SurveyMonkey, also allow for employee polling via e-mail. Some webcast and online meeting platforms also provide polling capabilities. It is so easy to conduct polls in the Digital Age that organizations must be concerned with bombarding their employees with too many polls.

Organizations also need to be concerned with the quality of the data they receive from online polls. Unlike telephone polls conducted by professional researchers, online polls are open access; participants are self-selected, and therefore, the results aren't statistically valid. For one thing, employees without computer access won't be able to participate. In addition, the information collected also may lack context and likely will require follow-up research.

While the data may not be statistically valid, polls can provide you with a glimpse of employee attitudes and help to determine employee interest in a subject. For instance, a poll question might ask employees what topics they would like to see discussed on the next company-wide webcast or which employee benefits they rate the highest.

Of course, an organization that wanted to conduct a statistically valid survey could do so by employing a professional research firm or by utilizing its own internal resources. For instance, organizations that have customer service call centers could use the customer service representatives to poll a random sample of employees. You could check with whoever oversees the call center to see whether its policy allows for such extra duty.

**Collecting Digital Analytics:** Intranets, e-mail and many other digital communication tools offer a wide range of opportunities for tracking and measurement. You can easily gather a multitude of quantitative data from your digital communications to identify trends and to measure activity and task completion. For instance, employees signing up for events online show participation trends, employees enrolling for their benefits online provide a real time measurement of action, and employees checking off the completion of a task using compliance software provide real time employee behavior data.

Most intranet platforms come with some built-in analytics showing such quantitative data as total page visits, unique user page visits, top-ranked pages, average time stayed on a page, highest usage times, top referring URLs and most common search phrases. In addition to built-in analytics, free analytical tools, such as Google Analytics, are available that may be able to track intranet user activity, depending on an organization's firewall configuration. You likely will need to work with your IT partners to configure intranet analytics.

A host of software is available for purchase that can help you manage blast e-mails, and most of these applications include analytics showing how many employees opened an e-mail and what links they clicked on from within the e-mail. Often an organization's marketing department is already using such e-mail management and tracking software, and sometimes that software can be used internally as well, perhaps at no additional cost.

While digital analytics can produce a multitude of data, it has to be analyzed. By collecting it on a cumulative basis, trends can be seen. Assumptions can often be made for some data, but additional research, such as an employee focus group, may have to be conducted to get a complete picture of what the data are representing. Let's see how that might work in an example.

Figure 10.5 shows an example of the monthly intranet unique user page visits for the fictitious ABC Airline. "Unique users" are individuals, so if an employee visits the intranet 10 times in a day, it only counts as once. This statistic tells the ABC employee communicators how many employees are using the company's intranet on a daily basis. By having the data displayed for the month, the communicators can see the usage trends. This particular month began on a Sunday, so the communicators know the large drops in visits are on weekends, and it is safe to assume that is because most employees aren't working on the weekends. The communicators decide to see what was on the home page on the fourth day of the month that created a small spike in visits; they discover there was an important message announcing a new route. They note that Thursdays have slightly more visits than other days of the week. They know from other data that the top ranked page on the intranet is the page where employees go to book their free travel. Like most airlines, ABC allows its employees to fly free if space is available. The communicators surmise that the small spikes on Thursdays are due to employees booking free travel for the upcoming weekend, but they would have to conduct further research to know for sure.

## Figure 10.5: ABC Airline Intranet Unique User Page Visits

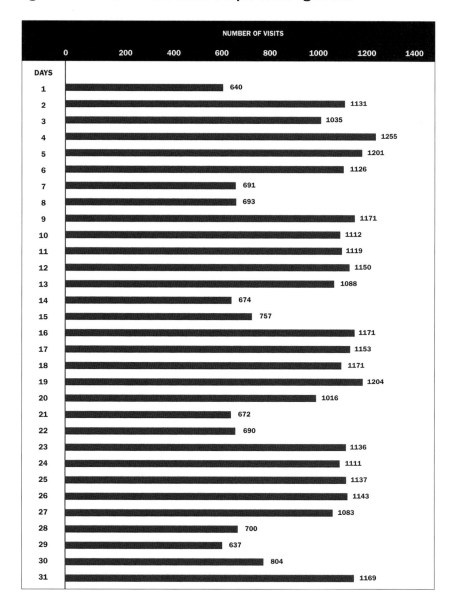

**Surveys:** Surveys provide employee communicators with a highly versatile tool to collect high-quality quantitative data through forced rankings and multiple-choice questions. In addition, by using open-ended questions or allowing for additional written comments, surveys can collect qualitative data.

Surveys can be distributed to employees online or as paper copies. Online surveys are relatively inexpensive to conduct and can provide instant results. Employees may be required to enter a survey control code to ensure they only take a survey once. Paper surveys can reach employees who do not have computer access, but printing and distribution of them can cost more and take more time to process. Once the surveys are returned, there are expenses related to collecting them and entering the results into a database.

While surveys are versatile, they do have limitations. Questions have to be worded carefully so they aren't misinterpreted. Unlike a focus group setting, surveys offer no opportunity to clarify questions or modify them for particular employees.

Questions also have to be worded in such a manner that employee communicators will know how to act upon the results the questions reveal (Sinickas, 2011). For instance, if a survey asks employees to respond to the statement "New webcasts should be made available once each quarter" and a majority of respondents disagree, you wouldn't know whether to increase or decrease frequency. A better way to phrase the question so the results are actionable is to list various options for frequency and ask employees to pick the one they think is right. So a good question would be, "Which of the following is best for you: weekly, monthly, quarterly?"

Many survey experts believe a 10-point Likert scale is needed to get enough differentiation in responses to get meaningful results. The 10-point scale asks for participants to rate their answer with 0 being the lowest, 5 being neutral and 10 being the highest. By contrast, the 5-point scale asks for participants to rate: 1. Very Unsatisfied, 2. Unsatisfied, 3. Neither Satisfied or Unsatisfied, 4. Satisfied, 5. Very Satisfied). In most companies, the vast majority of participants tend to answer with 4 and 5s and important differences are obscured. In addition to the 10-point scale, a 60% participation rate is recommended for accuracy. (Robert Berrier, Spring International, personal conversation, March 11, 2014).

Figure 10.6 includes some additional tips to help conduct a large-scale employee survey.

## Figure 10.6: Tips for Large-Scale Employee Surveys

| | |
|---|---|
| **Involve Employees** | • Establish a cross-functional steering committee to work with the survey vendor and manage the survey process.<br><br>• Establish Survey Captains representing every major workgroup to distribute control numbers and paper surveys, and to encourage participation. Choose Survey Captains who will be enthusiastic about the survey.<br><br>• To the extent possible, position the survey so employees feel like it is their survey, rather than management's survey. |
| **Campaign the Survey** | • Create a communication campaign for the survey to "get out the vote." Incorporate all existing communication channels and consider collateral such as posters, buttons and pens.<br><br>• Set a participation goal for the organization and update the results on a daily basis on a progress chart. The participation goal could be the percentage of the employee population needed for the survey to be statistically valid. The goal can be a rally cry. A button that says simply "72%" can generate buzz.<br><br>• Make sure survey participation results are updated where all employees can see them, such as on the homepage of the intranet and on sandwich boards by employee time clocks.<br><br>• Create a competition between workgroups to see who can generate the highest percentage survey participation.<br><br>• Workgroup leaders should visibly support the survey, and they should offer incentives for attaining survey participation goals. "I'll shave my head if we surpass our goal!" or "We'll have a pizza party for everyone if we meet our challenge!"<br><br>• Ensure survey confidentiality and integrity. |
| **Communicate the Survey Results** | • The survey findings must be summarized and communicated to the entire organization in clear and simple terms. Failure to do so will destroy organization credibility and future survey participation.<br><br>• Workgroup leaders should communicate results specific to their respective workgroups during town hall meetings.<br><br>• Celebrate the achievement of participation goals. |
| **Take Action** | • The organization must follow up on issues uncovered by the survey by developing and implementing action plans. Involve frontline employees in the development of the action plans. "You identified this problem; now help us fix it."<br><br>• Don't ask survey questions that the organization isn't prepared to follow up on. This erodes organizational credibility and future survey participation. |
| **Communicate Actions Repeatedly** | • Improvements and changes resulting from the survey must be communicated throughout the organization. Organizations often take action but fail to communicate the action adequately.<br><br>• One communication is not enough. Employee communicators should look for ways to remind employees several times over the course of 10-12 months following the survey about the actions resulting from the survey.<br><br>• Post a checklist of action plan items in a visible place. Update progress toward completion.<br><br>• Continue to use the survey steering committee and the Survey Captains to communicate the actions taken as a result of the survey. |

**Conducting Communication Audits:** To get the most complete and accurate picture of internal communication effectiveness, you will need to employ a third-party vendor to help conduct a communication audit. Because this process is time-consuming and expensive, it is usually only done in cycles ranging from one to five years.

The communication audit collects quantitative and qualitative data through the following methods:

- Research on previous measurement efforts, including those conducted by human resources that relate to leadership trust, organizational credibility, or employee morale, perceptions, attitudes, beliefs, commitment or engagement.

- Interviews with executive team leaders, department heads and other key individuals within the organization.

- Direct observation of key communication processes throughout the organization to ensure they are functioning properly and efficiently.

- Focus group meetings representing a cross-section of the organization.

- Online and paper surveys to reach as many employees as possible.

After collecting all the data, the vendor typically works with the employee communicators to put together a report of their findings and a list of recommendations based on the audit results. In many cases, the vendor will present the findings and recommendations to the organization's senior team. The vendor will explain the audit methodology, provide an analysis of the data, compare the results to peer companies, and present recommendations based on industry best practices and appropriate communication strategies. Recommendations, particularly those calling for increased spending on resources or staff, typically are better received coming from third-party experts than from internal staff.

# Measuring Engagement

As we discussed in Chapter 1, getting as many employees as you can to become as engaged as possible in your organization's success is the primary goal of effective internal communication. So how do you measure engagement?

First, we need to define what employee engagement is. For this book's purposes, employee engagement exists when an employee feels intellectually and emotionally connected to his or her work in such a way that the employee brings enthusiasm, intense focus and deep commitment to the success of his or her job and the organization.

To determine levels of employee engagement, researchers focus on these five employee areas: job satisfaction, organizational favorability, organization values, intent to stay and recommendation (Sue Oliver, Kantana Partners, personal communication, July 15, 2013). Figure 10.7 shows a potential survey question for each of those categories.

**Figure 10.6: Tips for Large-Scale Employee Surveys**

| CATEGORIES | POTENTIAL QUESTIONS |
|---|---|
| 1. Job Satisfaction | Rate your overall satisfaction as an employee: <br><br> 1   2   3   4   5   6   7   8   9   10 <br> Extremely Unsatisfied                          Extremely Satisfied |
| 2. Organizational Favorability | I feel proud to work for this organization. <br><br> 1   2   3   4   5   6   7   8   9   10 <br> Not At All Proud                          Extremely Proud |
| 3. Organizational Values | This organization lives up to its core values <br><br> 1   2   3   4   5   6   7   8   9   10 <br> Extremely Disagree                          Extremely Agree |
| 4. Intent to Stay | If I had it to do over again, I would join this organization. <br><br> 1   2   3   4   5   6   7   8   9   10 <br> Extremely Disagree                          Extremely Agree |
| 5. Recommendation | I would recommend this organization to family and friends as a great place to work. <br><br> 1   2   3   4   5   6   7   8   9   10 <br> Extremely Disagree                          Extremely Agree |

## Chapter Conclusion

If you want to be regarded as a strategic communicator and an executive counselor, you must focus on outcomes that are meaningful to your organization, and then find ways to demonstrate the effectiveness of your work to your internal clients and your senior leadership team. Too many internal communication professionals do great work but fail to communicate their successes. Just like any other communication campaign, you need to tell your story and trumpet your achievements. Apply the Six Cs to your evaluation report: make sure it is clear, concise, consistent, coordinated, credible and compelling. Look for creative ways to share your data and don't forget to sway hearts with anecdotal comments. The example shown in Figure 10.3 is one way to get results to busy clients and leaders in a format they can easily digest. Find what works for your organization.

Showing a little bit of swagger is OK, especially when it has solid data behind it. You do great work. You have a great story to tell. Make it shine!

## Chapter Exercises

Chapter Exercises

1. List three examples of qualitative data and three examples of quantitative data.

   _____

   _____

   _____

   _____

   _____

   _____

2. Assume you want to find out what employees' attitudes are about a recent change. What method(s) would you use to measure attitude? Write one generic question you would ask to reveal attitude.

   _____

   _____

   _____

3. Write a survey question for a fictitious organization to reveal what employees feel about the volume of e-mails they receive. Make sure all possible answers to your question are actionable by the internal communication team.

   _____

   _____

   _____

## Chapter References

Sierra, L. (2003). "Sierra's Theory of Communicativity." *Communication World,* 1(3), 38-40, 60.

Sinickas, A. (2011). "How to Use Communication Measures." *Communication World,* 9(10), 38-40, 60.

Sinickas, A. (2004). "The Top 10 Measurement Mistakes." *The Business Communicator,* 4(9), 8-9.

# Employee Communication Nirvana

"If we are to achieve results never before accomplished,
we must expect to employ methods never before attempted."
– Sir Francis Bacon

**N**ow that you have completed reading this book, hopefully you have discovered many templates, tools and proven practices that you can begin creating and using in your day-to-day work right away. Remember: for every hour it takes to develop one of the templates or tools, it will save you countless hours down the road. The templates and tools allow you and your team to execute tactics flawlessly, on time, on budget and on brand, which builds credibility with your organization's leadership and its employees. The deep thinking that goes into creating the templates and tools can be enlightening, and help you to see your work in new and exciting ways.

These templates and tools put you in a better position to react more quickly, and the proven practices help you to think more strategically and more creatively. Once you are unchained from the nitty-gritty details, you can focus on the proven practices and strategies presented in this book that can help you to find more powerful solutions to the complex communication challenges you are facing. Together, they form a foundation that allows breakthrough thinking to flourish and amazing results to happen.

So much can be gained by maximizing internal communication, but getting there is not easy. You will get there in stages, through hard work and by becoming more enlightened. There are no magic wands and no silver bullets. The path is fraught with bureaucratic pitfalls and obstacles along the way. You may stumble or lose momentum from time to time. But you must regain your footing and continue the quest. The ultimate goal is too important for you to quit; the ultimate reward too great to stop. You must lead your organization along this path—one step at a time.

I challenge you to take the first step today. There is no tomorrow. A long journey always begins with a single step. Here are 10 principles to guide you as you begin:

1. Devise rigorous processes that enable you to do your job flawlessly. Start with something simple like a written checklist for sending out a company-wide e-mail. Build from there.

2. Develop robust tools that lay a foundation upon which to build enlightened strategic communication plans. Use the communication channel matrix template in this book to develop a matrix for your channels.

3. Forge innovative communication plans that achieve a balance between art and science. Use the template provided in this book to start your own library of communication plans.

4. Make sure everything you create is aligned with your organization's business objectives and is in support of its vision. Start by making sure headlines and highly visible text echo verbiage from your organization's vision.

5. Become an effective strategic communicator and a trusted executive counselor. Understand the 20 Guiding Principles (see the following pages) and all their nuances and be prepared to discuss them with your executive leaders.

6. Be well-prepared for the inevitable crisis. It is going to happen and you will be the hero when you're prepared with pre-gathered materials and the powerful messaging outlined in this book.

7. Become a master at communicating change. Start by studying the tips for communicating change and understanding their practical applications in your organization. Adapt the change messages for your own organization.

8. Make sure your communication strategies deliver personal meaning and purpose for employees. Put yourself in their shoes. Always ask how any new change will affect them. What questions will they have?

9. Find measurable and meaningful results for your organization. Start small by keeping a running list of anecdotal evidence you collect. Devise simple but compelling ways to showcase your successes.

10. Focus on outcomes and continuously improve. Build upon your successes and replicate them. Never stop learning and trying to get better.

Always keep in mind where you're headed and always have fun in the pursuit of your dream. Celebrate your successes. Dream often. Dream big. See the vision in your mind so vividly that you can almost taste it, feel it, smell it. Ask yourself, "What does an organization that has maximized its internal communication function and fully engaged all of its employees look like?" I see such an organization as one that has gone through stages of enlightenment and attained a state of employee communication nirvana—the best that it can be.

Here's how I envision this organization:

- It has well-informed and deeply passionate employees.
- Business information is shared freely through highly efficient communication channels and well-designed networks.
- Open and honest conversations permeate the entire organization.
- Meaningful feedback mechanisms are embedded in the communication system.
- A high degree of trust exists between the organization's leaders and its employees. Its formal, semi-formal and informal voices are perfectly aligned. What the organization says it does aligns with what it actually does.
- Leaders and employees believe in each other.
- Employees are actively engaged in the organization's success.
- At all levels of the organization, employees are more concerned with "we" than "me."
- Employees understand where the organization is trying to go, how it is trying to get there and what their personal roles are in helping it to succeed.
- Communication is clear, concise, consistent, coordinated and compelling.

- Employees have better information to improve their own lives. They understand what it takes to get ahead in the organization. They have the information to make better career choices and personal decisions about their employee benefits options. They can create better lives for themselves and their families, and they can help their organizations succeed and prosper.

- This is what an organization that has achieved employee communication nirvana looks like, and this is what we are trying to achieve.

Finally, I invite you to contact me, share your stories of success and share which templates, tools, proven practices and strategies from this book or elsewhere best served you in your quest to maximize internal communication in your organization. My e-mail address is PaulBarton@Outlook.com.

I wish you the very best of luck in your pursuit. The opportunities have never been greater. The possibilities have never been more exciting. It is truly a great time to be an internal communication professional. Enjoy the journey!

*Paul Barton*

# 20 Guiding Principles for Internal Communication

1.  **Strategic communication helps a business achieve its objectives.** That is its purpose.

2.  **Effective internal communication produces meaningful results** and can be a competitive differentiator.

3.  **There are costs associated with communicating, but there can be costs associated with not communicating as well.** Internal communication professionals seek cost-effective and creative solutions to solve complex communication challenges.

4.  **Employees are drowning in information, but thirsting for understanding and purpose.** Our job is to make the important interesting. Help employees to filter and prioritize information.

5.  **Credibility is the foundation upon which effective communication is built.** Unless it is believed, a message has no worth.

6.  **Face-to-face communication is the most desirable form of communication because it is immediate, personal and interactive.** Most employees say their immediate supervisor is their preferred and most credible source of information about the business.

7.  **Communication is, by definition, a two-way process. Two monologues don't make a dialogue.** Meaningful feedback mechanisms must be part of every internal communication.

8.  **Leadership and communication are inextricably linked.** Employee communicators support organizational leaders by serving as consultants, facilitators and resource partners. The internal communication team is an organization's eyes and ears.

9.  **As in any effective strategy, form should follow function.** The medium is the message.

10. **Employees should learn of important events affecting them and their organization from an internal source rather than an external source.** Well-informed employees can serve as informal ambassadors of the organization.

11. **The more important the information is personally to the receiver, the fewer exposures are needed to make an impression.** Internal communication should be personally relevant to employees.

12. **True effectiveness in communication is the ability to influence and change behavior.** Changing behaviors is a long, slow process and, therefore, measurement of effective communication must be taken over time.

13. **Logic makes people think, but it takes emotion to make them take action and be moved to change.** It is more important to win hearts than minds.

14. **The case for change should be found in the marketplace.** For change to occur, employees must move through these stages: awareness, understanding, acceptance and commitment. You can't skip steps. Employees don't resist change; they resist being changed.

15. **Internal and external communication overlap.** Employees are informal ambassadors with customers and in the community so internal messaging should align with external strategies. Likewise, because employees see external sources, such sources are de facto employee communications and external messaging should align with internal strategies. Every internal communication must be written as if it will be read by external sources.

16. **Rumors are created to fill communication voids.** Fill those voids with valid information. Get in front of crisis and controversy. Establish internal communication as the trusted information source. A phrase like "We're aware of the problem, we're working on it and we'll keep you updated with any news" goes a long way to keep the rumor mill from grinding out of control.

17. **Well-defined communication processes and procedures are the foundation for breakthrough ideas.** Key message libraries, templates, crisis plans, checklists and other tools free up time for breakthrough thinking and continuous improvement.

18. **The overall tone of internal communication reflects the relationship an organization has with its employees.** The best tone for strategic communication is the Voice of the Brand, which is primarily what the company is but also what the company is striving to be. The Voice of the Brand is often a partnership tone.

19. **Timing is often a key element in maximizing effective communication.** When you say something is just as important as what you say.

20. **A common trait among successful organizations is open and honest communication with all their key audiences, especially their employees.** With better information, better business decisions can be made. Employees need to understand the "what" and the "why" to be engaged fully. Well-informed employees are more satisfied, more creative, more productive and more committed.

# About the Author

Paul Barton, ABC, is an author, professional speaker, employee communication consultant and entrepreneur. He has been passionate about internal communication for more than 20 years and has worked with numerous organizations to help them find creative, cost-effective solutions to complex communication challenges. Paul is a recognized leader in planning and implementing innovative communication programs to support large-scale initiatives, and in providing vision and counsel to help steer organizations through periods of organizational complexity. He has built internal communication functions from inception to successful operation and transformed languishing internal communication efforts into highly effective programs.

As a corporate communication professional, Paul led highly successful internal communication teams at Hawaiian Airlines, the nation's No. 1 on-time airline; PetSmart, the world's largest pet products and services company; America West Airlines (now American Airlines), one of the nation's fastest growing airlines; Phelps Dodge Corp. (now Freeport-McMoRan), the world's largest publicly traded copper mining and manufacturing company, and at Arizona Public Service, one of the nation's top-performing electric utilities and operator of the largest nuclear power plant in the U.S. Before beginning a career in corporate communications, Paul was a communicator at the American Compensation Association (now called World at Work), and he was a news editor at several small daily and weekly newspapers.

As a long-time member of the International Association of Business Communicators (IABC), Paul has won numerous IABC awards for his work, and he has earned the association's Accredited Business Communicator (ABC) designation. He has been a highly rated speaker by audiences at IABC, the Public Relations Society of America (PRSA), the Advanced

Learning Institute (ALI), World at Work, and the Employee Benefit Research Institute (EBRI).

Paul received a Bachelor of Science degree in Journalism and Mass Communication from Iowa State University in Ames, Iowa, in 1982, and he earned a Master of Arts in Communication from Hawaii Pacific University in Honolulu in 2013.

In 2013, Paul began his own communication consulting business specializing in internal communication. Paul and his wife, Maribel, have three children, Kaitlyn, Annamae and Joshua.

# About Paul Barton Communications, LLC

After a highly successful career in corporate communications spanning more than two decades, Paul Barton, ABC, decided in 2013 to fulfill a life goal by launching his own consulting firm, Paul Barton Communications, LLC.

The mission of Paul Barton Communications, LLC, is to work with clients to discover enlightened internal communication strategies that achieve meaningful results for their organizations and help enrich the lives of their employees.

Paul focuses on three areas:

- **Writing:** Contact Paul for bulk copies of this book, or requests for him to write guest blogs or articles.

- **Presenting:** Paul is available for keynote speeches and workshop presentations. He can customize an in-house workshop for your internal communication team.

- **Consulting:** Paul provides strategic communication counsel, coaching for key staff, custom in-house workshops and direct implementation support.

For a 30-minute complimentary consultation, contact Paul at PaulBarton@outlook.com.

# Internal Communication Consulting

**N**o one knows their businesses better than the clients themselves, so Paul Barton, ABC, believes consulting is a process done together in a mutually rewarding partnership. Paul works with clients and their teams, and together they create amazing results that could not be achieved without each other.

Paul is available to work with you and your team on retainer or for specific project work. He provides strategic counseling, coaching for key personnel, custom in-house workshops, and project implementation support.

Paul works with clients who:

- Need fresh employee communication ideas, or expertise and support for a specific project or internal communication campaign.

- Are implementing a major internal initiative and need employees to get on board and adopt change quickly.

- Want to strengthen trust and commitment among the workforce.

- Are looking for new communication approaches to ensure employee benefit offerings are properly utilized and highly valued by employees.

- Need a written crisis communication plan that allows them to manage the inevitable crisis effectively, and helps their organization recover as fully and quickly as possible.

- Want to use social media and new communication technologies to reach and engage diverse employee groups.

# Connect with Paul

Paul Barton, ABC, believes social media is a great way to create an ongoing dialogue, and augment and enhance personal and business relationships. Here's how you can connect with him:

- Website and blog: paulbartonabc.com
- Facebook: www.facebook.com/PaulBartonCommunicationsLLC
- Twitter: www.twitter.com/PaulBartonABC
- Google+: https://plus.google.com/+PaulBartonABC/posts
- LinkedIn: http://www.linkedin.com/in/paulbartonabc

# Book Paul Barton to Speak at Your Next Event

When it comes to choosing a professional speaker for your next event, you'll find no one more respected or more knowledgeable in the field of internal communication than Paul Barton, ABC. After hearing one of Paul's high-energy presentations, audience members are inspired by the communication philosophies he presents and many say they can't wait to get back to the office to try the practical approaches he offers.

Whether your audience is 10 or 10,000, in North America or overseas, Paul can deliver a tailor-made message of enlightenment and inspiration to business leaders, HR managers and communication professionals. Paul's style of speaking combines his real life experiences at five of the nation's fastest growing companies with his intense passion and quick wit to deliver an enlightening and entertaining presentation.

Paul has been a highly rated speaker by audiences at the International Association of Business Communicators (IABC), the Public Relations Society of America (PRSA), the Advanced Learning Institute (ALI), World at Work, and the Employee Benefit Research Institute (EBRI).

If you are looking for a presenter who will both inspire and inform, then book Paul Barton today.


## What Attendees are Saying about Paul Barton, ABC, as a Presenter

*(taken from speaker rating forms)*

"Great examples and very entertaining."

"Will be fun to share these ideas with my team."

"Wow! Great! Very thought-provoking!"

"Entertaining speaker and different approach to communication.
Very creative and fun."

"Lots of good ideas and just enough humor."

"Excellent! Easily the 'Robin Williams' of this conference."

"Tremendous energy and fun."

"Solid content ideas and gave me lots to think about."

"Inspires us to think outside the box."

"Great job! The No. 1 speaker at the conference!"

"Creative, fun, unique, practical, useful."